MEMORY PALACE DEFINITIVE

James Smith

THE NUMBER-LETTER CODE

is pretty much the basis of the palace and techniques such as the "Dominic System" [see *numbers and letters (strings of)* in **MEMORY IMPROVEMENT TOPICS A-Z**] for memorising combinations of numbers and letters. In the number-letter code, numbers are converted into letters and vice-versa, thus allowing the memoriser to make words from any combination of numbers, and numbers out of any combination of letters:

Number	Associated Letters			
0	**o**	t		
1	**a**	u		
2	**b**	l	v	
3	**c**	k	m	w
4	**d**	x		
5	**e**	y		
6	**f**	p	s	z
7	**g**	j	q	
8	**h**	r		
9	**i**	n		

Letters highlighted in **bold** are the most habitually used and would therefore be my first choice for interchanging with the associated number. Where this might present conceptual difficulty, as will become clearer as we explore the system, the other letters associated within the code with that number are defaulted to.

0   the letter **o** resembles the number **0**; t is the 20th letter of the alphabet

1   **a** is the **1**st letter of the alphabet and has **1** downstroke; u the 21st

2   **b** is the **2**nd letter of the alphabet, l the 12th, v the 22nd and consists of **2** lines

3	c is the 3rd letter of the alphabet, **k** has the same sound as a hard **c** and consists of **3** lines; m is the 13th letter of the alphabet and contains **3** downstrokes, w the 23rd and has **3** of both tips and interior corners
4	d is the 4th letter of the alphabet, x the 24th and has **4** limbs
5	e is the 5th letter of the alphabet, y the 25th
6	f is the 6th letter of the alphabet, p the 16th, s and z start respectively with the *s*ame and near-identical *s*ound as **6**
7	g is the 7th letter of the alphabet, j has the same sound as a soft **g** and q is the 17th letter of the alphabet
8	h is the 8th letter of the alphabet, r the 18th
9	i is the 9th letter of the alphabet, the letter n is in the spelling of **9**

I would recommend familiarising oneself with the NLC, as we will be calling the number-letter code henceforth, where possible, until thinking with it feels natural; perhaps with copies:

* pasted onto your desktop
* kept around - say, in your wallet - for regular perusal

and during free time:

* testing yourself by first covering the letters then revealing after answering
* recording and then playing back repeatedly, perhaps on headphones while between work and home, a technique easily done with any other aspect of memorisation (see **MEMORIZING YOUR MATERIAL AND REVISION**).

I would also note down your own ways of memorising the associations between each number and letter. And of course you may well want to revert to revising the NLC later as the overall principles become habitual.

BUILDING A MEMORY PALACE: LOCATIONS FOR PAGES, OBJECTS FOR KEYPOINTS

Each Location has been generated according to the NLC code. Thus for Location **2**, I would first use a Location whose name begins with the letter **b**, our first choice for that number, giving us the following possibilities I find most memorable and easiest to visualise:

Bank
Barn
Basement
Bathroom
Bedroom
Bedsit
Bungalow

As per the NLC code, our second choices in order, for the number **2** are the letters l and v, yielding the following further possible locations I find most memorable:

Library
Lighthouse
Lobby
Loft
Lounge
Ocean **L**iner
Tower of **L**ondon

then, for v:

Vineyard

and thus for, example, for locations of two digits (or page number) **31**

(state or country capitals given in brackets):

CAlifornia (Sacramento)
Close-**U**p
MAssachusetts (Boston)
Metropolitan **A**rea
OMA (**OMA**n; Muscat)
WAshington (Olympia)
Wide-**A**ngle

(number of examples from **LOCATIONS 0-999** reduced to save space)

Death **S**tar (*Star Wars*)
Deck **P**lans
Deer **P**ark
Dental **S**urgery
Department **S**tore
Doctor's **S**urgery
Duty **F**ree

(number of examples from **LOCATIONS 0-999** reduced to save space)

and for those locations/pages of three digits such as **708**:

GOR (setting for series of fantasy novels by John Norman; intj. used as a mild oath)

JORdan (Amman)

or **950**:

Near-**E**arth **O**bject
NET

(number of examples from **LOCATIONS 0-999** reduced to save space)

I have included as possible Location combinations that may seem overly abstract or absurd but perusing these will help to fix the NLC code in your long-term memory, develop your vocabulary and may, as we shall see in my examples, be most memorable to you, possibly in their oddity.

Each Location or page of text has been populated using the NLC system with a standard set of 100 possible Objects, each of which is designed to be associated with a key "chunk" of information and which can be modified or added to as need be, so 100 should be ample for most study purposes. Examples for Object number **5**:

Elevator
Enclosure
Envelope
Escalator
Espresso
to**E**
to**Y** (for these last two examples, rather quirkily, the letter t is the default letter for the number 0 so is ignored; and **Y** respectively count

for the number **5**)

(number of examples from **OBJECTS 0-99** reduced to save space)

Object **36**:

Card Slot
Cattle Prod
Ceiling Fan
Ceiling Sprinklers
Key Pad
Mail Slot
TCP
Wall Panel
Wall Safe
Water Fountain
Water Pipe

(number of examples from **OBJECTS 0-99** reduced to save space)

PLEASE NOTE: you do not have to memorize every option in these two lists but use them whenever you need to memorize! I also give you later, both as examples and for even ongoing easy use, **10 SAMPLE LOCATIONS AND OBJECTS.** But browsing **LOCATIONS 0-999** and **OBJECTS 0-99**, especially as one starts using them for study, forms a useful alternative to and a way of more fruitfully using such habits as reverie with happy memories associated with things in the Lists and fascinating but mindless habits such as browsing on the Internet or inane chat and saving money on, say, long-winded vacations or naive fantasy fictions. The human brain usually seeks out the *new* and to reflect; the boredom you may feel from merely browsing each Location and Object per se - or once each of these two has been associated in your long-term memory with material you wish to remember - should be resolved when you associate the new material you need to learn with it.

Students of foreign languages may save study time and strengthen their understanding by writing in translation alongside or testing themselves against the Locations and Objects, especially once they are using for study or work in a memory palace.

Chunking makes the most efficient use of the short-term memory in decreasing the number of items for recall by increasing the size or importance of each item. Thus, the sight or even concept of a fetish may initiate torrid feelings of sexual anticipation (perhaps repressing intimacy and preventing satisfaction) while negating other accessorial turn-offs, credit card numbers are split into groups of four and telephone numbers [for my preferred system for memorizing these, please see: numbers and letters (strings of) under **MEMORY IMPROVEMENT TOPICS A-Z**] into several such. Chunking is the conscious association of seemingly meaningless or difficult-to-assimilate information with memorable things stored in your long-term memory.

Similarly, I tend to use mind mapping [see especially online (currently: *thinkbuzan.com/iMindMap*) and *The Mind Map Book* by Tony Buzan] as a reasonably efficient method of summary and cross-referral (see my comment immediately prior to the heading **SUGGESTED NON-LINEAR WAYS OF PRESENTING REVISION MATERIALS**), believing much of its usefulness comes from the mental initiative and fluid intelligence necessary to create the map. Within your maps, as shall soon become clearer, you may wish to note page numbers with Locations and even Objects for key points.

Tony has also produced a definitive list of the 12 principles of memorization, which may be chunked as the acronym *SMASHIN' SCOPE*:

1.   Sensuality/Synaesthesia. Most of the habitual memorizers and all of the great mnemonists developed, like Dr. Lector in Thomas Harris's novels, an increased sensitivity in each of their senses and kinesthesia (your consciousness of bodily position and movement in space) then chunked or blended these senses to enhance recall

2.   Movement adds another huge range of possibilities for your brain to 'tune in' and recall. I have "embodied" my viewing and playing of my deepest interests in soccer, weight training and so forth in my memory skills. As your images move, make them 3-D and detailed

3.   Association. Link whatever you need to remember to something in your mental environment or long-term memory

4.   Sexuality. I use pretty much most of the women I fancy, making a note when they have sprung to mind, everything I used to find or still find arousing (hasn't changed) and erotic humor

5.   Humor and Fun. Play with the most absurd, surreal or morbid things that spring to mind or that you can recall

6.   "Imagination is limited embraces the entire world, stimulating progress, giving birth to evolution ... Imagination is more mportant than knowledge ... For knowledge is limited" - Einstein. The more imagination you bring to memorizing, the better your memory will be

7.   Number adds specificity and efficiency to the principle of order and sequence

8.   Symbolism. Substituting a more meaningful image for a more banal or dry one increases the probability of recall

9.   Color. Make creative, not necessarily "realistic" play with the full spectrum. Like in media, you may want to play with color, contrast, shadow etc. I do not recall ever dreaming in monochrome, even as "quotation"

10.   Order and/or Sequence permits much more immediate reference and increased the brain's possibilities for 'random access'

11.   Positivity/the Pleasure Principle: positive and pleasant mages are usually better for memorizing because the brain will naturally want to return to the images. Similarly, negative and unpleasant ones tend to be memorable when presented in humor or tragedy

12.   Exaggeration. Tends to come naturally in images in terms of their selection and relativity and size, shape and sensuality.

[rewritten from pages 10 and 11 of *Master Your Memory* (David and Charles, 1989) by Tony Buzan by kind permission of the author, *www.thinkbuzan.com*]

Playing with all of the **SMASHIN' SCOPE** principles as with film grammar, you may visualize and sound things in multiple "planes" or in fluid "play", slow, reverse or random motion (see **MEMORIZING YOUR MATERIAL AND REVISION**), juxtapositions, superimpositions, incongruities, ironies, reverse or random motion, various tempos and rhythm or music filling the room or around the Objects etc. The sequences I recall with most pleasure and interest from films have been set to the most remarkable music which I collect and which recall, among other pleasurable associations, the Locations themselves. And needless to say, allow them full play (and take notes of memorable things as they occur to you) when thinking up Locations and Objects (perhaps different from my very full list of suggestions) you would prefer to use.

I would strongly recommend finding out as soon as possible precisely what material you will need to know for your job, an exam etc., and start memory-palacing it. With work, you may be able to obtain as full a list of instructions ahead of training in addition to your own notes and records (an acquaintance working in IT keeps a database in *FoxPro* of the more important previous problems and solutions, should they occur again) and reading lists are often issued ahead of classes. If they have not been, I would strongly recommend asking your tutor for one or at least to recommend texts or sections of relevance. Upon mempalling your notes, which should be kept together and in general mempal order, they should be reviewed regularly in comparison with the original texts to be studied to maintain understanding and recall. As most books consist of way too much verbiage and are sometimes repetitively written so even causing confusion, you will also around this time be developing skills in recognizing and meaningfully reorganizing information of quality and relevance.

As I mentioned in **THE NUMBER-LETTER CODE**, you may even wish to dictate the keypoints of the most difficult to recall material from the memory palace or, to a lesser extent, the original text and replay to yourself, perhaps on headphones, while during otherwise vacant everyday chores like preparing meals, household work, taking transport or even at the gym.

MEMORIZING A SINGLE PAGE OF MATERIAL BY ASSOCIATING CHUNKED KEYPOINTS WITH MEMORY PALACE OBJECTS

You may always wish to keep a copy of this book on your person, or at least **LOCATIONS 0-999** and **OBJECTS 0-99** while studying material you will probably need to mempal.

1. Use a study copy with sufficient blank space for note-taking, preferably in pencil

2. If not done already, number the page of the material - books, photocopied originals, your own notes etc. - you need to memorize

3. Write the Location (or combination of - chunked - Locations) from **LOCATIONS 0-999** (or suchlike most memorable to yourself: for further suggestions, see **GENERATING YOUR OWN LOCATIONS 100-999** and **GENERATING LOCATIONS 1000-9999**) that matches the page number of the text to be remembered next to this page number. If you are committing to memory, say, a lot of material on a page number **2**, you might for variety, put Objects 1 through 50 in the **B**asement and the rest in the **L**oft

4. Study the text and underline or highlight all keypoints you need to know, usually as the most memorable chunks of key syllables, words or symbols (this includes discerning the relevant from verbiage; generally speaking, the more concisely written the text, the more difficult it is to apply memory techniques)

5. Bracket off each section of these keypoints (you should become better at this with practice) you feel you can retain as one memorable chunk (or mind map, even a small one if that works best)

6. Attach in numerical order the Object (or Objects) from

OBJECTS 0-99 or an original Object or combination thereof that for you can most memorably [and which probably suits the Location(s) chosen in step 3] be associated with each bracketed-off chunk

If you are memorizing at short notice, you may wish to choose the Location and Objects that most immediately spring to mind or that you have already been using - perhaps those immediately around you - against which you may most easily test yourself

7.   Add in, if you feel you need to, further brief notes - images, a very short story, anything to turn the sometimes very dry into the memorable - that will help you to recall each section of text, or write these on a separate sheet of paper for study with your notes.

If you find mempalling rather monotonous, get stuck, simply move to the next section of text to be memorized and follow the preceding seven steps; you can always return to "fill in" the more difficult passages after inspiration or discussion.

If, for instance, you had to memorize this entire section of text for discussion in an exam (reproduced by kind permission of Dr. Paul Coates, to whom I have given a complementary copy of this book, from page 131 of his *The Realist Fantasy*, Palgrave Macmillan, 1983):

The theological implication of the self-sufficiency of this world is that

it has been given over to the demonic, which – and this is the measure

of the story's equivocation and ultimate failure – may or may not be

the human irrational. The place of the master has been usurped by the servant: Mrs Grose reports that that Quint used to wear the master's

waistcoats; and just after the governess has wished to see the master

she glimpses Quint above her (in the position of the master) at the

tower window. The Quint-Master relationship resembles that between

the real and the symbolic body of the king in medieval political

theory: the one subject to corruption, the other lodged in ideal glory.

Behind James's use of the motif of the double body lies the theme of

the double itself. The loss of the master is what Derrida would term

the loss of the Ultimate Signified, the accent of dominance.

When the governess first sees Quint a complicity between their looks is implied; he 'seemed to fix me, from his position, with just the

question, just the scrutiny, through the fading light, that his own

presence provoked'. The exchange of looks is like an exchange of

places. On the second occasion when she observes Quint, as he stares

at her through a downstairs window, she rushes out after him:

It was confusedly present to me that I ought to place myself where he

had stood. I did so; I applied my face to the pane and looked, as he

had looked, into the room. As if, at this moment, to show me exactly

what his range had been, Mrs. Grose, as I had done for myself just before, came in from the hall. With this I had full the full image of a

repetition of what had already occurred. She saw me as I had seen my

own visitant.

And on the third occasion on which she sees Miss Jessel – she is

accompanied by Mrs Grose and Flora – she remarks that the

apparition 'rose erect on the spot my friend and I had lately

acquitted.'

At the end of section XV she witnesses the image of a woman seated

writing as if to her lover, and naturally enough, at the end of section

XVI, she herself sits down to write to the master she would like to have as a lover.

These quotations indicate the extent to which the pattern of looks built

up by The Turn Of The Screw *is based on substitution and projection.*

The degree to which the governess is unconsciously jealous of Miss

Jessel, who possesses the master-substitute Quint, is evident in her

unwillingness to name the rival; she does not name her when she first

sees her, and later she sees only the back of her apparition, head

bowed, at the foot of the stairs. As she considers the other from

behind, the back is an image of her own alienated self. (Compare the

Munch paintings of or the films of Antonioni).

2.   If not done already, number each page of the materials - books, photocopied originals, your own notes etc. - you need to memorize:

131

The theological implication of the self-sufficiency of this world is that

it has been given over to the demonic, which – and this is the measure

of the story's equivocation and ultimate failure – may or may not be

the human irrational. The place of the master ...

(rest of example text left out for concision)

3.   Write the Location (or combination of - chunked - Locations) from **LOCATIONS 0-999** (or suchlike most memorable to yourself: for further suggestions, see **GENERATING YOUR OWN LOCATIONS 100-999** and **GENERATING LOCATIONS 1000-9999**) that matches the page number of the text to be remembered next to this page number:

131 ADVANCED CARGO AIRCRAFT

The theological implication of the self-sufficiency of this world is that it has been given over to the demonic, which – and this is the measure

of the story's equivocation and ultimate failure – may or may not be

the human irrational. The place of the master ...

(rest of example text left out for concision)

4. Study the text and underline or highlight all keypoints you need to know, usually as chunks of the most memorable key syllables, words or symbols:

131 ADVANCED CARGO AIRCRAFT

*The **theo**logical **implic**ation of the **self-suff**iciency of this world is that*

*it has been **given over** to the **demon**ic, which – and this is the **measure***

*of the story's **equiv**ocation and ultimate failure – may or may not be*

*the **human** irrational. The place of the **master** has been usurped by*

*the **servant**: Mrs Grose reports that that Quint used to wear the* *master's waistcoats; and just after the governess has wished to see the*

master she glimpses Quint above her (in the position of the master) at

the tower window. The Quint-Master relationship resembles that

between the real and the symbolic body of the king in medieval

political theory: the one subject to corruption, the other lodged in

ideal glory.

(rest of example text left out for concision)

5.   Bracket off each section of these keypoints (you should become better at this with practice) you need to know you feel you can retain as one memorable chunk:

131 ADVANCED CARGO AIRCRAFT

The [theological implication of the self-sufficiency of this world is *that it has been **given over** to the **demon**ic], which – and this is the*

*[**measure** of the story's **equiv**ocation and ultimate failure – may or*

*may not be the **human** irrational]. The place of the [**master** has been*

*usurped by the **servant**: Mrs Grose reports that that Quint used to*

*wear the **master's waistcoats**; and just after the governess has wished*

*to see the master she glimpses Quint above her (in the **position** of the*

***master**) at the **tower window**]. The Quint-Master relationship*

*resembles that between the [**real** and the **symbolic body** of the King in*

*me**die**val **pol**itical **theory**]: the one subject to [**corruption**, the other*

*lodged in **ideal glory**]*

6. Attach in numerical order the Object (or Objects) from **OBJECTS 0-99** or an original Object or combination thereof that for you can most memorably [and which probably suits the Location(s) chosen in step 3] be associated with each bracketed-off chunk:

131 ADVANCED CARGO AIRCRAFT

1 Ashtray

The *[theological **implication** of the **self-sufficiency** of this world is*

*that it has been **given over** to the **demonic]**, which – and this is the*

2 Light

*[**measure** of the story's **equivo**cation and ultimate failure – may or*

*may not be the **human** irrational]. The place of the [**master** has been*

*usurped by the **servant**: Mrs Grose reports that that Quint used to*

3 Ceiling

*wear the **master's waistcoats**; and just after the governess has wished*

*to see the master she glimpses Quint above her (in the **position** of the* *master) at the **tower window***]. *The Quint-Master relationship*

4 trap Door

*resembles that between the [**real** and the **symbolic body** of the king in*

5 Elevator

*me**dieval pol**itical **theory**]: the one subject to [**corruption**, the other*

*lodged in **ideal glory**].*

6 Floor

*Behind James's use of the [**mot**if of the **double body** lies the **theme** of*

7 Grill

*the **double**] itself. The [**loss** of the **master** is what Derrida would term*

*the **loss** of the **Ultimate Signif**ied, the **accent** of **dom**inance].*

8 Handrail

*When the [**governess first** sees **Quint** a **compl**icity between their looks*

*is im**plied**]; he 'seemed to [**fix** me, from his position, with **just** the*

9 oN button

question, *just the* **scrut**iny, *through the fading light, that his own*

10 Advanced Technology

presence provoked']. The [exchange of **looks** *is like an exchange of*

11 AA phone

places]. On the [second occasion when she observes Quint, as he

stares *at her through a* **downsta**irs **window]**, *she rushes out after him:*

12 Air Vent

*It was [***confusedly present*** *to me that I ought to* **place** *myself where he*

had **stood]**. *I did so; I applied my face to the pane and looked, as he*

had looked, into the room. As if, at this moment, to show me exactly

*what his range had been, Mrs. [***Grose**, *as I had done for myself just*

before, came in from the hall. With this I had full the ***full image*** *of a*

~ 23 ~

13 oAK

*repetition of what had already occurred. She **saw** me as I had seen my*

*own **visitant].***

*And on the **[third** occasion on which she sees Miss Jessel – she is*

accompanied by Mrs Grose and Flora – she remarks that the

14 †AX

*apparition '**rose erect** on the **spot** my friend and I had **lately***

*ac**quitt**ed.]'*

*At the end of section XV she witnesses the **[image** of a **woman** seated*

15 American Eagle

*wri**ting as if to her **lover**, and naturally enough, at the end of section*

*XVI, **she herself]** sits down to write to the master she would like to* *have as a lover.*

These quotations indicate the extent to which the [pattern of looks

16 †AP

built up by The Turn Of The Screw *is based on substitution and*

projection]. The degree to which the [governess is unconsciously

17 †AG

jealous of Miss Jessel, who possesses the master-substitute Quint], is

evident in her [unwillingness to name the rival; she does not name

18 †AR

her when she first sees her, and later she sees only the back of her

apparition, head bowed, at the foot of the stairs]. As she considers the

[other from behind, the back is an image of her own alienated self.

19 †AN

(Compare the Munch paintings of or the films of Antonioni)].

7. Add in, if you like, further brief notes - images, a very short story, anything to turn the sometimes very dry into the memorable - that will help you to recall each section of text or write these on a separate sheet of paper for study with your notes:

131 ADVANCED CARGO AIRCRAFT

1 Ashtray

In (perhaps picture this as a scenario in miniature) or around the **1 Ashtray**, a man called **Theo**, while **self**(-consciously) suffering, **gives over pli**ers to a **demon**

2 Light

Under **2 Light**, a **measure** near a **quiver** (or perhaps being stretched out and held by a human hand **quiver**ing in fear) of a **human rat** or **rat**ions

3 Ceiling

Under or perhaps seen from a low angle so that the **3 Ceiling** is ominously prominent, a **servant** dissolves into the position of a **master** while wearing the **master's waistcoats** he has always worn, at a **tower window**

4 trap Door

is flung open on the deck, to reveal an enclosure in which rests with a **cymbal** on top **body** of a **diva** in **polyth**ene

5 Elevator

Probably on a far wall of the **131 Advanced Cargo Aircraft**, linking the cargo area we are looking around to the rest of the plane, the **5 Elevator** door **rupt**ures (breaks open) to reveal the **dealt glory** of a winning hand (at cards)

6 Floor

We hear the sound of an aircraft **mot**or through the floor (can aurally link the sounds of the first syllable of the word *motor* with the first letter in **6 Floor**), slightly juddering a **double body** (two dead) on top of a **thimb**le

7 Grill

in the **7 Grill**, the **master**, who resembles some **Ultimate Sign**, is

lost (though still recalled in negation) with his **domina**ting **accent** or the accent of a dominator

8 Handrail

easy to recall: simply picture next to the **8 Handrail**, which typically run along the length of the interior of **131 Advanced Cargo Aircraft**, the **governess** and **Quint first** seeing each other with im**plied comp**licity (**plie**rs and **comp**ost, bearing in mind the psychological factors in the narrative of sadomasochism, animalism and shared bodily needs, spring to mind here)

9 oN button

Links between the chunks: **9 oN-fix-sit-just-quest** and the final two as sononyms: **screw-presents-poked**. One's contextual understanding of their association probably make this section most memorable in its bizarre suggestiveness and "unmemorability"

10 Advanced Technology

Easy to imagine some **10 Advanced Technology**, perhaps a hybrid and speculation of what you've witnessed in some futuristic fantasy or in the news, and like in competition there are always ex**change**s of **looks** and **places**

11 AA phone

Perhaps like in some **131 Advanced Cargo Aircraft**, the **11 AA phone** might be attached to the wall for crew communications or it could be part of the cargo. Next to it, or perhaps when we are using it, the governess's **seconds** are drawn out in nightmarish terror as she observes Quint **star**ing at her through a **downstairs window**. Given the governess' sexual repression, fears of assault and hysteria, the association of fear with **downstairs** may have significance, too

12 Air Vent

In the **12 Air Vent**, most likely spotted when one looks to the ceiling of the **131 Advanced Cargo Aircraft**, the bizarre image of a **confused present place**d on the **stud** of a rivet

13 oAK

Perhaps a piece of grossly (thickly) varnished **13 oAK** being shipped in the aircraft. In its reflection, you might see the (substitution story?) **full**, conscious **image** of Mrs Grosse seeing the governess as she might see her **own visit**ant

14 †AX

Bundled **14 †AX** forms being mailed: **third** of a batch of **roses** (taxingly) **erect**s on a **spot late**ly ac**quit**ted by the storage personnel

15 American Eagle

Under an **15 American Eagle** logo on the wall of the aircraft, or perhaps on the table she is writing upon, we see the **image** of Jessel **writ**ing to her **lover** Quint and simultaneously envisaged, yet happening in real time at the end of the section, the governess doing the same

16 †AP

easy to associate probably a running **16 †AP**, perhaps part of the upper wall of the cargo plane, its cascade forming a **pattern** of **looks** over a miniature **sub**marine and a **proj**ector

17 †AG

Difficult like the **9 oN** section most memorable the chunks for me to link would be: **17 †AG-gov-unconsc-jeal-Jess-mast-subst-Quint**

18 †AR

Difficult like the **17 †AG** section, would choose to play with **17 †AG-unwill-name-first see-later-back-foot-stairs**

19 †AN

Perhaps appearing **19 †AN** under the lighting conditions and shadows of the interior of a loaded **131 Advanced Cargo Aircraft** and because of the assumption that threats are of a different appearance, easily to link: **other - image** of her own **alien self**, perhaps (disgust is a basic human reaction in fear) **munch**ing **ant**s

MEMORIZING SEVERAL PAGES OF MATERIAL BY ASSOCIATING CHUNKED KEYPOINTS WITH MEMORY PALACE OBJECTS

1. Use a study copy with sufficient blank space for note-taking, preferably in pencil

2. If not already so done, number each page of the materials - books, photocopied originals, your own notes etc. - you need to memorize

3. Write the Location (or combination of - chunked - Locations) from **LOCATIONS 0-999** (or suchlike most memorable to yourself: for further suggestions, see **GENERATING YOUR OWN LOCATIONS 100-999** and **GENERATING LOCATIONS 1000**) that matches the page number of the text to be remembered next to this page number. If you are committing to memory, say, a lot of material on a page number **2**, you might for variety, put Objects 1 through 50 in the **L**oft and the rest in the **B**asement

4. Study the text and underline or highlight all keypoints you need to know, usually as the most memorable chunks of key syllables, words or symbols (this would include discerning the relevant from a text's verbiage; generally speaking, the more concisely written the text, the more difficult it is to apply memory techniques)

5. Bracket off each section of these keypoints (you should become better at this with practice) you feel you can retain as one memorable chunk (or mind map, even a small one if that works best)

6. Attach in numerical order the Object (or Objects) from **OBJECTS 0-99** or an original Object or combination thereof that for you can most memorably (and which probably suits the Locations chosen in step 3) be associated with each bracketed-off chunk

If you are memorizing at short notice, you may wish to choose the Location and Objects that most immediately spring to mind or that you already use in your memory palace - perhaps those immediately around you - against which you may most easily test yourself

7. Add in, if you feel you need to, further brief notes - images, a very short story, anything to turn the sometimes very dry into the memorable - that will help you to recall each section of text, or write these on a separate sheet of paper for study with

your notes.

Here is how, for example, I would memorize the entire section *3.3.2 Engine Failure at Altitude*, which runs from pages 32 to 33 in *Aircraft Operating Instructions (AOI) ASTM Compliant Flight Manual Apollo Delta Jet AS-III912S Revision 1* by Abid Farooqui, who has also received a complimentary copy of this book:

32

If the engine stops while operating at cruise or full power when the

aircraft is well clear of the ground, proceed as follows:

Establish Glide Speed

Select Landing Area

Proceed to Landing Area

NOTE: For establishing best glide your attention is drawn to section

5.5.1 of this manual

Check the following:

Fuel Contents

Carb Icing (Turn Carb Heat On -> Optional -> New models optioned

with carb heat have it automatically on all the time)

Fuel Valve Off

Ignition On

Choke Off

Continue with the rest of emergency landing procedure as listed in

this section:

33

If your engine fails in flight, do not attempt to restart the engine

unless one of these items is found to be incorrect and is able to be

rectified. Relax and maintain control while concentrating on correct

emergency landing techniques.

Adopt a suitable glide speed preferably with a tail wind. With a tail

wind, minimum sink speed would give you the longest glide. As a

careful pilot, you should always fly in "a cone of safety", at sufficient

altitude, with an understanding of the orientation of the wind. It is not

enough to simply land on the area of choice. **REMEMBER** *to account*

for the possible obstacles that you could discover only at the last minute (e.g. power lines, ditches etc...) and ground related and/or

mechanical turbulence that may occur. Check that your seat belt and

that of the passenger is securely fastened.

The final approach should be made preferably into the wind. With the

onset of night the approach should be with the sun at the rear if

possible. Your aircraft will be quiet, check that there is nobody on the

ground. Make a short landing run if possible. If you have time, you

can try to start the engine again whilst in flight. Verify that the

problem is not from a memory lapse: choke lever actuated, fuel valve accidentally off, carb icing, ignition switches off... Remember, even if

the engine starts again remains in the cone of flight safety and land on

the area initially considered, so as to determine the possible origin of

*the engine failure **BEFORE** continuing the flight.*

3. Write the Location (or Locations) from **LOCATIONS 0-999** (or an invented one most memorable to you) that matches the page number of the text to be remembered next to this page number (for more choice in choosing a Location most memorable to yourself, see sections **GENERATING YOUR OWN LOCATIONS 100-999** and **GENERATING LOCATIONS 1000-9999**):

32 CELL BLOCK

If the engine stops while operating at cruise or full power when the

aircraft is well clear of the ground, proceed as follows:

Establish Glide Speed

(rest of example page left out for concision)

33 MISTY MOUNTAINS

If your engine fails in flight, do not attempt to restart the engine

unless one of these items is found to be incorrect and is able to be

rectified.

(rest of example page left out for concision)

4. Study the text and underline or highlight all keypoints you need to know, usually as the most memorable chunks of key syllables, words or symbols:

32 CELL BLOCK

If the engine stops while operating at cruise or full power when the

aircraft is well clear of the ground, proceed as follows:

Establish Glide Speed

Select Landing Area

*Proceed to **Landing Area***

NOTE: For establishing best glide your attention is drawn to section

__5.5.1__ of this manual

Check *the following:*

(rest of example page left out for concision)

33 MISTY MOUNTAINS

*If your engine fails in flight, do **not** attempt to **restart** the **eng**ine*

***unless one** of these items is found to be **inc**orrect and is able to be*

*rectified. R**elax** and **maintain** **cont**rol while **concen**trating on correct*

*emergency **landing techniques**.*

(rest of example page left out for concision)

5.   Bracket off each section of these keypoints (you should become better at this with practice) you feel you can retain as one memorable chunk:

If the engine stops while operating at cruise or full power when the

aircraft is well clear of the ground, proceed as follows:

[Establish Glide Speed]

[Select Landing Area]

[*Proceed to* **Landing Area]**

NOTE: For establishing best glide your attention is drawn to section

<u>5.5.1</u> of this Manual

[Check] *the following:*

(rest of example page left out for concision)

33 MISTY MOUNTAINS

If your engine fails in flight, do [not attempt to restart the engine

unless one of these items is found to be incorrect and is able to be

rec]tified. [Relax and maintain control while concentrating on

correct emergency landing techniques]

(rest of example page left out for concision)

6. Attach in numerical order the Object (or Objects) from **OBJECTS 0-99** or an original Object or combination thereof that for you can most memorably (and which probably suits the Locations chosen in step 3) be associated with each bracketed-off chunk:

32 CELL BLOCK

If the engine stops while operating at cruise or full power when the

aircraft is well clear of the ground, proceed as follows:

[Establish Glide Speed]   1 Ashtray

[Select Landing Area] **2** *Book*

[Proceed to **Landing Area]** **3** *Cupboard*

NOTE: For establishing best glide your attention is drawn to section

<u>5.5.1</u> *of this manual*

[Check] *the following:* **4** *Duvet*

[Fuel Contents] **5** *Elevator*

[Carb Icing (Turn Carb Heat On -> Optional -> New models

6 *Sill*

*optioned with carb heat have it **automatically** on **all** the **time)]***

[Fuel Valve Off] **7** *Glass*

[Ignition On]   8 Ramp

[Choke Off]   9 oN button

[Continue with the rest of emergency landing procedure as listed in

10 Access Opening

this section]:

33 MISTY MOUNTAINS

If your engine fails in flight, do [not attempt to restart the engine

11 Analogue-to-Analogue

unless one of these items is found to be incorrect and is able to be

rec]tified. [Relax and maintain control while concentrating on

12 HUB

correct emergency landing techniques].

13 oAK

[Adopt a suitable glide speed preferably with a tail wind]. With a tail

14 toAD

wind *[minimum sink speed would give you the longest glide]*. As a

15 Air Entry

careful pilot, you should *[always fly in "a cone of safety"]*, at

16 tAP   *17 tAG*

[sufficient altitude], with an *[understanding of the orientation of the*

wind]. It is not enough to simply land on the area of choice.

18 oAR

REMEMBER to account for the *[possible obstacles that you could*

19 tAN

discover only at the last minute]* (e.g. *[power lines, ditches etc...])* and

20 Body Odor

[ground related and/or mechanical turbulence] that may occur.

21 BA

Check that your seat *[belt and that of the passenger is securely* *fastened]. The [**final approach** should be made **preferably into the***

wind]. *With the [**onset** of **night** the approach should be with the **sun** at*

*the **rear** if **possible]. Your [aircraft** will be **quiet**, check that there is*

nobody *on the **ground]**. Make a [**short landing run** if **possible]**. If you*

*have [**time**, you **can try** to **start** the **engine** again whilst in **flight]**.*

*[**Verify** that the problem is not from a **mem**ory **lapse]**: [**choke lever***

actuated], *[**fuel valve** accidentally **off]**, [**carb icing]**, [**ignition***

switches off]...*Remember, even if the engine starts again remains in*

*the [**cone of flight** safety] and [**land** on the area **initially considered**,* *so as to **determine** the **possible origin** of the **engine failure BEFORE***

*con*tinuing *the flight].*

7.   Add in, if you feel you need to, further brief notes - images, a
     very short story, anything to turn   the sometimes very dry
     into the memorable - that will help you to recall each section
     of text, or write these on a separate sheet of paper for study
     with your notes:

32 Cell Block

1 Ashtray

in the **1 Ashtray**, probably on a guard's desk as prisoner smoking
may be restricted, the image of **stab**bing (cutting) **glid**ing (as it spills
from the **1 Ashtray**) **speed** (amphetamines)

2 Book

very easy to recall this; essentially "by the **2 Book**." Computer
readout **select**ion of a **landing area** within the pages of an open book
(see also: *33 Misty Mountains 33 Cruise Missile*)

3 Cupboard

within, image of **seed** leading to or falling upon (perhaps growing
cress) the **landing area**

4 Duvet

belonging to a guard on night duty or a prisoner, upon which lies an
open **check**

5 Elevator

(for guard use only and connecting the various levels of the guards-
only areas of the prison) its doors open and a torrent of **fuel cont**ents,
perhaps flailing with guards spills forth; the rather acrid smell of
diesel **fuel** increasingly permeating the *32 CELL BLOCK*

6 Sill

on the high **6 Sill** of a cell, would take up **carb**ohydrates to reach the **icy** sill, we see **new models auto**matically on with carb icing frosting their sides

7 Glass

on the heavy frosted **7 Glass** of a cell window, the **fuel valve** is **off**

8 Ramp

Perhaps sloping up to barred gates through which prisoners and guards must pass to enter of leave the block, we see an **igni**ted **8 Ramp**

9 oN button

Release the **Choke 9 oN button** - and it's **off**

10 Access Opening

Perhaps a contactless delivery tray or a head-hole in a cell door; link the keywords: **cont-rest-merge-land-seed-this sex**

33 Misty Mountains

11 Analog-to-Analog

engine not restarted unless one **ink wreck**ed/knocked over and spilt

12 HUB

relaxing and in control in the **12 HUB** (perhaps a bright day in the *33 Misty Mountains?*) while you **concen**trate on **merg**ing (playfully pressing together into fun, recognizable forms) **land** or mud, using **techniques**

13 oAK

Diving into deep water from an **13 oAK** overlooking it in an **adopt**ed **suit**, you **glide** with **speed** after **preferring** a **tail wind**

14 toAD

a **14 toAD** keeps a **minimum sink speed** to give itself the **longest glide** into deep water

15 Air Entry

Diving from a rocky wall in one of the *33 Misty Mountains* into deep water, behind which an **15 Air Entry** shaft keeps you in a **cone** of **safety** from falling back onto rock

16 tAP

under a natural **16 tAP**, a mountain wall perpetually spurting a small amount water into a lake, fish - like salmon - jump to **altitude**

17 tAG

as you stand, a **17 tAG** of your clothing blows in the **orien**tal (easterly) direction of the **wind**

18 oAR

at the or until the last minute, you try to clear a **possible obstacles** (*33 Misty Mountain* rocks) with an **18 oAR**

19 tAN

against a **19 tAN** sky and a generally light brown environment, looking up from a **ditch** towards the **power lines** passing over

20 Body Odor

ground and **mech**anical **turb**ulence brings out all your **20 Body Odor**. We can clean up upon landing

21 BA (eternal soul in Egyptian mythology; degree)

pilot and passenger **belt**s (maybe picture catastrophe here during a rough descent if you don't) to save our souls or it doesn't take a degree to realise the need to do this

22 Bunk Beds

preferring the **final approach** to be made **into the wind**, the plane perhaps passing between enormous wind-buffeted **22 Bunk Beds** in mid air

23 Bar Code

onset of **night** easy to picture; **sun**light at the **rear** perhaps diffused through an enormous interpolated **23 Bar Code**

24 *outward Backward Downward* (path of the facial nerve in the facial canal)
the facial nerve connects the **quiet aircraft** to **nobody** on the **ground**

25 *Bevel End*

landing run short, like the length of a **25** *Bevel End*

26 *LP*

picture this suggestion coming from an **26** *LP* being played - or the engine starting up, if you have the time, like an **26** *LP*

27 *Bungee Jump*

Verify - carefully check - or like a **27** *Bungee Jump* in which the head is knocked, **mem**ory **lapse** could ensue

28 *BoreHole*

Easy to picture: **choke lever actuated**, pulled from a slot rather like a **28** *BoreHole*

29 *oBI* [African sorcery (obeah); to bewitch]
by **29** *oBI* [African sorcery], the **fuel valve** is **off**

30 *Chimney Tray*

Carb icing in a **30** *Chimney Tray*

31 *Magic User*

a **31** *Magic User* **offs** the **ignition switches**

32 *toMB*

a **32** *toMB* shaped like a **cone of flight** - or we're less likely to end up in a **32** *toMB* soon enough if we stay in a **cone of flight**

33 *Cruise Missile*

a **33** *Cruise Missile* **land**s harmlessly into a **land niche**; easy to then picture, as we know this is the last stage of this set of instruction, **determining** the **possible origin** of the **engine failure before cont**inuing the flight (see also *32* *Cell Block 2 Book*)

Keypoints with relevant Locations and Objects from other parts of the texts or other texts can simply be cross-noted.

SUGGESTED NON-LINEAR WAYS OF PRESENTING REVISION MATERIAL

1.   akin to mind mapping, e.g.:

16 TRACK AND FIELD

1 Ashtray	**2** Baton	Billboards	**3** Coach	Microphones
			time Clock	Wind
4 Discus		**5** Elevator	Escalator	**6** Podium
7 Javelin	Triple Jump	**8** Hurdles		**9** I
10 toUT	**11** (resembles parallel posts)		**12** Air Bag	
13 Access Card Arm Chair	**14** Automatic Doors	**15** American		
		Eagle		
16 US	**17** Arcade Game	**18** tAR	**19** tAN	
20 Body Odor	Box Office	**21** VU (view)	**22** Breeze	
			Blocks	
23 Bronze Medal	Broom Cupboard	Vacuum Cleaner etc.		

2.   grid paper (with squares large enough to contain each Object and material you're associating it with)

3.   a plan or map of each actual Location you are using. User-friendly maps or plans for business high-rises, campuses, city centres, cruise ships, major hospitals, malls and theme parks, for example, are easily obtainable or printable from the Net and easily blown up and reproduced by scanning or photocopying.

To memorize, for example, a diagram 3.4 in a text, you may, with reference to **OBJECTS 0-99**, chunk the keywords in the diagram around your depiction image of a **CD** (object **34** in the list, roughly equating 3.4 with the number 34) . For a diagram 3.4.2, perhaps chunk with a **CD** (object **34**) and a **L**ight (object **2**) or a **W**all (object **3**) with a **D**ry **B**ulb (object **42**) attached to it.

Fluid intelligence: the system I give you is merely a tool with suggestions. Play with it and run with what works best for you. You may, for instance, quite obviously not wish to associate a Location with a page number using the NLC but as a central or associated with a subject image in a mind map

CONTINUING TO USE THE SAME LOCATIONS AND EVEN OBJECTS FOR FURTHER TEXTS

If you later needed to have a working knowledge of the following passage for an exam discussion (and thus need to recall the page number as citation) as well as this passage from *The Story of the Lost Reflection* (Verso, 1985), again reproduced by kind permission of its author, Paul Coates, I quoted in **MEMORIZING A SINGLE PAGE OF MATERIAL BY ASSOCIATING CHUNKED KEYPOINTS WITH MEMORY PALACE OBJECTS:**

The films of Andrei Tarkovsky are an extraordinary fusion of the desolation and the ecstasy of the mystic. *Stalker* bursts into color the moment the stalker enters the Zone; the lone extra-societal region in which he feels at home; and yet this region is also the depressive landscape seen as characteristic of allegory by Walter Benjamin: it is littered with ruined objects, as behaviorally disturbed as the mind of the stalker himself - of which it is a mirror and an allegorical objectification. At the end of the film, both stalker and viewer are left doubting the efficacy of the Zone: if no-one is prepared to enter the room in which, it is said, one's most inmost desire is fulfilled, may it not be that, as well as fearing the explosive hidden contents of their own minds, everyone also fears that the room may be a shrine 'whereof the saint is out' - banished, to put it crudely, by the black magic of an officially atheist society?

The Zone in *Stalker*: the planet that materializes the thoughts of those who observe it in *Solaris*: both are mirrors of the minds that apprehend them. So it is not surprising that the most central, conceptually unified, desolate and movingly epiphanic film in Tarkovsky's canon should be entitled just that: *Mirror*. The mirror is not 'a mirror to one's times', as many critics have stated. Rather, it is that which, on the one hand, reverently upholds the object by carefully repeating it, and on the other, destroys the aura of the object by reproducing it, by removing it from itself: as a film removes the face of reality and allows it to be transported elsewhere. The mirror effects an exact and delicate balance of absence and presence.

This passage also occurs on page 131, the same as the passage for memorization from *The Realist Fantasy*. In this case, as there is no obvious logical continuation to the material, I would note the final Object used to chunk material from that passage - **19 †AN** - then continue to memory palace this passage from Object **20**, which you would select from **OBJECTS 0-99**:

Bird **T**able
Blow **T**orch
Body **O**dor
Booby **T**rap
Box **O**ffice
Burn**O**ut
Lap **T**op
LO!

or use one of your choosing, and so forth.

If, in the unlikely instance you use up all 100 Objects in one Location:

* use a different Location for each new text or set thereof. Thus, if you have already used a **H**ide **O**ut and 100 Objects for page **80**, or just want a new Location for the sake of variety and surprise, you may wish to continue using the **R**ound **T**able (Camelot) and environ and fresh Objects for ensuing material

* (and you wish to continue using the same Location) restart from Object number 1, as long as you don't confuse yourself by chunking too much information from different sources at the same Location and Object.

To reduce the repetitiveness and possible slight increase in confusion of using the same or similar Objects, you may wish to try: with Location 1, of course start with Object 1. But with Location **2**, start with Object **2** (or even object **21**), Location **3** Object **3** (or even object **31**), and so on.

However, when continuing to use the memory palace to recall instructions, I would match each instruction number in turn with its equivalent number from **OBJECTS 0-99**.

If, for instance, the light aircraft instructions I showed you one way to memorize in the section **MEMORIZING A SINGLE PAGE OF**

MATERIAL BY ASSOCIATING CHUNKED KEYPOINTS WITH MEMORY PALACE OBJECTS were part of a hobby, you worked with Tower Cranes as your first job and you had to memorize from section 3 - 2 (let's call it page 32) of the *Tower Crane Reference Manual*:

9   Operate the crane only if all *protective* and *safety devices* are in place and fully functional

10   Before starting up the crane, make sure that nobody can be *endangered*

11   Before beginning work, make sure you make yourself familiar with the circumstances of the site ...

(instructions 12-18 left out for concision)

I would use Objects 9 through 11 and from section 3 -3 (page 33):

19   *Maintain the safety distance*: min. 0.5m

20   Keep the safety instructions and warnings attached to the crane always *complete* and *perfectly legible*

21   *Malfunctions:*

*   *Stop* the crane *immediately*
*   Have any defects *rectified immediately*

(rest of page left out for concision)

MEMORIZING YOUR MATERIAL AND REVISION

After a one-hour period of study you should review your material:

approximately after:	Approximate Review Period (in minutes)
30 minutes (following a 10-minute break)	10
24 hours	2-4
1 week	2
1 month	2
6 months	2
1 year	2

Like the assistance-free conditions of an exam or at work, best start with a quick self-test without revising the material to see what you recall. You may then check or keep a note against the original materials, adjusting any discrepancies, noting new ideas and strengthening any areas of weak recall.

If any locations you are using for memorisation are in your immediate area, such as your **3** **K**itchen or **66** **S**wimming **P**ool, walking round these and testing each object in turn against your notes should add extra dimensions to your learning.

To continue building your confidence, you may also test yourself mentally against Locations and Objects you are using for recall.

Implement where not distracting from more relevant work, as I began to suggest in **THE NUMBER-LETTER CODE**, Locations and Objects of your choice into your daily life, so you may test yourself against the list (in order of importance) of things to do at work in your planner or on your shopping list.

LOCATIONS 0-999

I have included nouns, acronyms and roots that seem less usable choices but which match the NLC and Locations easily suggested by the letter combination for each number but which do not seem to be in official use - e.g. **ASY**lum for Location **165**. Each of the world's countries has been classified according to its three-digit Olympic code and respective capital in brackets; US states by zip and capital. Brackets also emphasize the most important definitions for words and acronyms and suggest Locational or situational ideas for that number.

0	0-shaped circuit
0	Observatory
0	Office
0	Oilfield
0	Opera
0	Orchard
0	Outpost
0	Tavern
0	Temple
0	Terrace
0	Thunderstorm
0	Tornado
0	Trailer
0	Train (first digit of Objects 10-99 denotes each carriage number in turn; the second, the number of each Object)
0	Treetops
0	Tundra
0	Turnpike
1	Abattoir
1	Airport
1	Airship
1	Annex
1	Arcade
1	Archive
1	Astroturf
1	Atlantis
1	Atrium
1	Attic
1	large construct resembling a 1 such as the Washington Monument
1	Trans Am
2	Bank
2	Barn
2	Basement
2	Bathroom
2	Bedroom
2	Bedsit
2	Bungalow
2	Lagoon
2	Lawn
2	Library
2	Lighthouse
2	Lobby
2	Loch
2	Loft
2	Lothlorien, Middle-Earth

2	Lounge
2	Ocean Liner
2	Thames Barrier, London
2	Tower of London
2	Vineyard
3	Cafe
3	Castle
3	Catacombs
3	Caverns
3	Cellar
3	Commissary
3	Compound
3	Condominium
3	Conservatory
3	Cottage
3	Kitchen
3	Mall
3	Maze
3	Mill
3	Mirkwood, Middle-Earth
3	Moorland
3	Multiplex
3	Museum
3	the OC (Orange County)
3	OKlahoma (Oklahoma City)
3	tennis Court
3	Tyrell Corporation (*Blade Runner*)
3	Warehouse
3	Watchtower
3	Windmill
3	Woodland
4	Docks
4	Dungeon
4	opium Den
4	Temple of Doom (*Indiana Jones*)
4	TX TeXas (Austin)
4	X-Wing Fighter (*Star Wars*)
4	Xanadu
	yacht (resembles a 4)
5	Ecstasy (state of)
5	Embassy
5	Energy
5	Estuary
5	Pentagon
5	Y-Wing Fighter (*Star Wars*)

5	Yard
5	YMCA/YWCA
6	Factory
6	Farm
6	Favella, 281 BRAzil
6	Ferry
6	Forum
6	Foundry
6	Freeway
6	Funfair
6	oil Field
6	Old Forest, Middle-Earth
6	open Plan
6	OZ (*Wizard of*)
6	Palace
6	Party
6	Port
6	Promenade
6	online Shopping
6	Séance
6	Shrine
6	Stables
6	Stargate (*2001: A Space Odyssey*)
6	Street
6	Studio
6	Study
6	Supermarket
6	Swamp
6	Trafalgar Square, London
7	Garage
7	Garden
7	Ghetto
7	Greenhouse
7	Gulch
7	Jungle
7	Junkyard
7	Olympic Games
7	ToGo (Lome)
8	Hairdresser
8	Hallway
8	Hangar
8	Heaven
8	Hell
8	Hospital
8	House

8	Hypermarket
8	OHio (Columbus)
8	ORegon (Salem)
8	Railroad
8	Rainbow
8	Ranch
8	Rave
8	Refinery
8	Refuge
8	Restaurant
8	Revolution
8	Riot
8	River
8	Rooftops (city, evening)
8	Ruins
8	tea Room
9	Infirmary
9	Island
9	Neighborhood
9	Newsfloor (789 JouRNalism)
9	Nursery
9	TN TeNnessee (Nashville)
10	Administration Office
10	Adults Only
10	Alton Towers (theme park), England
10	Arctic Ocean
10	Atlantic Ocean
10	UTah (Salt Lake City)
11	AA (rough, cindery lava)
11	Alcoholics Anonymous
11	Amusement Arcade
11	Assembly Area
	two large parallel constructs such as monuments resembling an 11
11	Urban Area
12	Air Base
12	ALabama (Montgomery)
12	Arch Bridge
12	Arctic Base
12	Arnhem Bridge, 954 NED (Netherlands; *A Bridge Too Far*)
12	Asteroid Belt
12	TUValu (Funafuti)
12	U-Boat
12	Underground Lair

13	AirCraft
13	Aircraft Carrier
13	AK AlasKa (Juneau)
13	Alternating Current (stretches of pylons)
13	AM
13	Upper Class (typical residence thereof)

14	Active Directory (Microsoft-created technology providing a variety of network services)
14	ADvertisements (location proliferating in them)
14	AeroDrome
14	Anno Domini
14	Archaeological Dig
14	Underwater Diving

| 15 | Accident and Emergency |
| 15 | Atrocity Exhibition (kind of slang for the mass media) |

16	Airlift Squadron
16	Artist's Studio
16	AZ AriZona (Phoenix)
16	Track And Field
16	Under Siege
16	Underground Shelter
16	US

17	AGriculture
17	Airlift Group
17	Art Gallery
17	tUG

18	Amityville House (*The Amityville Horror*)
18	ARkansas (Little Rock)
18	toUR
18	TURkey (Istanbul)
18	Utility Room

19	Alcatraz Island, USA
19	Ascension Island (728 GBR mid-Atlantic military airfield)
19	TANzania (Dodoma)
19	TUNisia (Tunis)
19	United Nations

20	Back Office
20	Bell Tower
20	Bermuda Triangle
20	Lecture Theatre

20	Looney Tunes
20	Lunar Orbit
20	oBO (a vessel that can trade with oil, bulk and ore cargoes)
20	VT VermonT (Montpelier)

21	Bowling Alley
21	Los Angeles
21	LA LouisianA (Baton Rouge)
21	VA VirginiA (Richmond)

22	Bacteria Beds (percolating filters at a sewage works)
22	Beam Bridge
22	BLock
22	Botany Bay, 116 AUStralia (also name of spaceship stranded on windswept barren planet 315 Ceti Alpha 5 in *Star Trek II*)
22	Bree, Lothlorien, Middle-Earth
22	Las Vegas

23	Barbican Centre, London
23	Basketball Court
23	Bates Motel (*Psycho*)
23	Before Christ
23	Benedictine Monastery
23	Berlin Wall, 758 GERmany
23	Best Western
23	Border Crossing
23	Bumper Cars
23	Leisure Centre
23	Level Crossing
23	Lincoln Cathedral, England
23	Log Cabin
23	Luxury Coach
	Network **23** Building (*Max Headroom: 20 Minutes Into The Future*)
23	Virgin Megastore

24	Barrow-Downs, Middle-Earth
24	BirthDay
24	BounDary
24	La Defense, Paris

25	Bag End, Middle-Earth
25	Land's End
25	toBY [(thieves' slang) the road]

26	Baseball Field
26	Battle Zone
26	Big Sur, 31 CAlifornia

26	Boarding School
26	Book Shop
26	Building Site
26	Building Society
26	Bulk Storage
26	Bus Station
26	Landfill Site
26	Liquor Store
26	Log Flume
26	London Planetarium
26	Love Shop (free swinger's palace in *Logan's Run*)
26	TLS Timor-Leste (Dili)
27	BarGe
27	BattleGround
27	Battlestar *Galactica*
27	B&Q (728 GBR hardware supermarket)
28	Beverly Hills, 31 CAlifornia
28	Bicycle Race
28	Black Hole
28	Board Room
28	Boat House
28	Borley Rectory, England
28	Burnt House
28	Laundry Room
28	Lost Highway
28	Vacation Resort
28	Village Hall
28	Virtual Reality
29	BI- (two; plane)
29	Book Inventory
29	LaNe
29	Omaha Beach, Normandy, 681 FRAnce (shore landing sequence of *Saving Private Ryan*)
29	Vancouver Island, 319 CANada
30	Channel Tunnel
30	Circus Tent
30	COlorado (Denver)
30	CT ConnecTicut (Hartford)
30	Cycling Track
30	Minas Tirith, Middle-Earth
30	MO MissOuri (Jefferson City)
30	MT MonTana (Helena)
31	CAlifornia (Sacramento)

31	Close-Up
31	MAssachusetts (Boston)
31	Metropolitan Area
31	OMAn (Muscat)
31	Tower of Cirith Ungol, Middle-Earth
31	WAshington (Olympia)
31	Wide-Angle

32	Cantilever Bridge
32	Cell Block
32	Chicago Loop, 92 ILlinois
32	Children's Bedroom
32	Colorado Lounge (*The Shining*)
32	Master Bedroom
32	Moon Base
32	WV West Virginia (Charleston)

33	Call/Contact Centre
33	Car Chase
33	City Centre
33	Cloud City (*The Empire Strikes Back)*
33	Comedy Club
33	Country Club
33	Medical Centre
33	Middle Class (typical residence thereof)
33	Mission Control
33	Misty Mountains, Middle-Earth
33	Off World Colony (*Blade Runner*)
33	TKM TurKMenistan (Ashgabat)
33	Working Class (typical residence thereof)

34	**3-D**
34	Castle Dracula
34	Christmas Day
34	MD Maryland (Annapolis)
34	Mass Destruction
34	Millennium Dome, London
34	Mount Doom (active volcano with ashen slopes, caverns and molten lava pit), Middle-Earth

35	Country Estate
35	KY KentuckY (Frankfort)
35	ME/MY (Objects related to or owned by self)
35	ME MainE (Augusta)
35	Mos Eisley (*Star Wars*)
35	Mount Everest, 956 NEPal
35	Mountain Express
35	**WE**

| 35 | WYoming (Cheyenne) |

36	Camp Site
36	Caravan Site
36	Central Park
36	*Chocolate Factory*
36	Clothing Store
36	Coffee Shop
36	Cold Storage
36	KS KansaS (Topeka)
36	*Mansfield Park*, England
36	Monaco Palace, 309 MONaco
36	Mother Ship
36	Mountain Peak/Slope
36	MS MiSsissippi (Jackson)
36	Multi-Storey
36	OCP (*Robocop*)
36	Wall Street
36	Wembley Stadium (now demolished), London

37	Card Game
37	Cheddar Gorge, England
37	Computer Graphics
37	County Jail
37	Crazy Golf
37	Miniature Golf
37	Winter Games

38	Capitol Hill/White House
38	Cargo Hold
38	Carnegie Hall
38	Changing Room
38	Cloak Room
38	Computer Room
38	Concert Hall
38	Conference Room
38	Convalescent Home
38	Mental Hospital
38	Miniature Railway
38	Mirrored Room
38	Motel Room
38	Mountain Range
38	Total Control Racing
38	War Room (*Dr Strangelove*)

39	Cave Network
39	Channel Islands, England
39	Concrete Island

39	**MI**chigan (Lansing)
39	**MN** Min**N**esota (Saint Paul)
39	to**WN** (-house)
39	**WI**sconsin (Madison)
40	**D**eep **O**cean
40	**D**esk**T**op
40	**D**iesel **T**rain
40	**DO** (local social event usually including refreshments)
40	**D**own**T**own
40	**D**rive-**T**hrough (including restaurant)
40	**D**rop **T**ower
41	**D**ark **A**ges (roughly, the period of both cultural and economic deterioration and disruption that took place in Western Europe following the decline of the Roman Empire and which includes the Arthurian period)
41	**D**isaster **A**rea
41	**DU**plex (a two-unit apartment building or condominium)
41	o**DA** (harem room)
42	**D**ata **B**ase
42	**D**eath **V**alley
42	**D**igital **B**attleground
42	**D**isney**L**and
42	**D**ou**B**le (Objects doubled, perhaps in a perpendicular or vertical mirror)
42	**D**ragon's **L**air
43	**D**etention **C**enter
43	**D**isney**W**orld
43	**D**og **K**ennel
43	**D**riving **C**ourse
43	Washington **DC** (formally the **D**istrict of **C**olumbia)
44	**4-D**
44	**D**ry **D**ock
44	**D**ungeons & **D**ragons
44	**D**unkin' **D**onuts
44	**D**urin **D**oors (Mines of Moria entrance), Middle-Earth
45	**D**ata **E**ntry (large office of PCs and data entry workers)
45	**DE** [(Latin) God; of, from: entity of god-like powers; place of worship]
45	**DE**laware (Dover)
46	**D**eath **S**tar (*Star Wars*)
46	**D**eck **P**lans

46	Deer Park
46	Dental Surgery
46	Department Store
46	Desert Plain
46	Doctor's Surgery
46	Duty Free
46	Dyson Sphere (encompassing structure orbiting a star to capture most or all of its energy output and also reflect it back to in-between inhabited satellites, perhaps constructed of demolished rocks from an outer planet's core)
47	Dark Galaxy (hypothetical galaxy-sized object held together by dark matter containing few or no stars)
47	Disc Golf
47	Disc Jockey (broadcasting studio)
47	Discussion Group
48	Day Hospital
48	Death Row
48	Delivery Room
48	Dining Room
48	Dressing Room
49	Desert Island
49	Digital Network
49	DowN (-slope; *Watership*)
49	Drive-In
50	Eiffel Tower
50	Enemy Territory
50	Yukon Territory (abounds with snow-melt lakes, pine forests and perennially snow-capped mountains), 319 CANada
51	Employment Agency
51	Enemy Aircraft
51	European Union
51	Evacuated Area
52	Encyclopaedia Britannica
52	Ewok Village (*Return of the Jedi*)
52	tEL (ancient mound in the Middle East)
53	East-West
53	Endless Corridors
53	Emergency Ward
53	Yacht Club
53	Youth Club

54	EDucation (school, college, university etc.)
54	EX- (former, out of)
55	Eagle Eye
55	Electrical Engineering
55	Elementary Education
	Highway 55
55	Youth Encounter
56	Egyptian Pyramids
56	Elevator Shafts
56	Engine Shop
56	Evacuation Zone
57	Equipment Ground
57	tEG (yearling sheep)
57	Year Group
58	Emergency Room
58	Entrance Hallway
58	Escape Route
58	Exhibition House
58	Youth Hostel
59	Easter Island (southeastern 60 Pacific Ocean, famous for its eight-hundred and eighty-seven extant monumental statues)
59	ENemy (Objects used as target practice)
60	Ferry Terminal
60	Pacific Ocean
60	Pearson Towers (apartment building in *Fight Club*; location was Promenade Towers, 21 LA)
60	Post Office
60	Shanty Town
60	*Solaris* (1972) Ocean
60	Southern Ocean
60	Subway Train
60	toFT (homestead; hillock; name of several English villages)
60	toPO [(coll.) a pic of a mountain with climbing routes superimposed on it]
60	Zoom Out
61	PA PennsylvAnia (Harrisburg)
61	Pile Up
61	Picnic Area
61	Poltergeist Activity
61	Salvation Army

61	Schloss Adler (mountaintop castle in *Where Eagles Dare*; Schloss Werfen, 110 AUT Austria doubled)
61	Silent Area
62	FLorida (Tallahassee)
62	Sick Bay
62	Silicon Valley
62	Split Level
62	Super Bowl (with distance markings for Objects)
62	Surfing Beach
62	Suspension Bridge
63	Final Cut (editing software)
63	Paris Metro
63	Pennine Way, England
63	Piccadilly Circus, London
63	PM
63	Pompidou Centre, France
63	Press Conference
63	Prison Camp
63	Sennan Cove, England
63	Sewage Works
63	Shopping Mall
63	SC South Carolina (Columbia)
63	Sistine Chapel, Italy
63	Space Mountain, Disneyland
63	Sports Centre
63	Squash Court
64	Fire Department
64	Police Department
64	Public Domain
64	Scuba Dive
64	SD South Dakota (Pierre)
64	Semi-Detached
64	Space Dock
64	Star Destroyer (*Star Wars*)
64	Store Display
65	Foreign Exchange
65	Scrap Yard
65	Ship Yard
65	Space Elevator (from planetary surface to orbit)
65	Stroboscopic Effect
65	Stock Exchange
65	Storage Yard
65	TPE Chinese TaiPEi (designated name used by 389 CHN to refer to Taiwan; Taipei City)

66	*Fantastic Planet* (1973)
66	Fashion Parade
66	Flag Ship
66	Food Farm
66	Football Pitch (with distance markings for Objects)
66	Forest Plantation
66	oPerationS
66	Pelennor Fields, Middle-Earth
66	Pine Forest
66	Pinewood Studios, England
66	Prancing Pony, Middle-Earth
66	Pumping Station
66	San Francisco
66	Service Station
66	Shopping Precinct
66	Soccer Pitch
66	Solar Sailor (*Tron*)
66	Space Port
66	Space Station
66	Space Shuttle
66	Subway Station
66	Swimming Pool
67	Shooting Gallery
67	Spaghetti Junction (69 Stack Interchange)
67	Zero Gravity
67	Zoological Gardens
68	Firing Range
68	old People's Home
68	Panic Room
68	Polar Region
68	Pool Hall
68	Public Relations
68	Shower Room (group)
68	Ski Run
68	Skywalker Ranch
68	Spare Room
68	Stock Room
69	Parris Island (Marine training), 63 SC South Carolina
69	Planetarium Inside
69	Private Investigations
69	Stack Interchange (67 Spaghetti Junction)
69	Space Needle, 31 WAshington
69	Zoom In

70	Ghost Town
70	Ghost Train
70	Gran Turismo
70	Greyhound Track

71	General Assembly
71	GeorgiA (Atlanta)
71	Jesus Army
71	T**GA** Ton**GA** (Nuku'alofa)

72	*Ghost Busters*
72	Good Vibrations
72	Great Lakes, 161 USA and 319 CANada
72	Green Belt
72	Jodrell Bank, England
72	Train a Grande Vitesse, 681 FRAnce

73	Games Workshop
73	Gardening Center
73	Glamis Castle, Scotland
73	Golf Course
73	Gotham City (*Batman*)
73	Grand Canyon
73	Job Center
73	T**JK** Tajikstan (Dushanbe)

| 74 | Garbage Dump |
| 74 | Grand Duchy (territory ruled by a grand duke or grand duchess) |

| 75 | Grave Yard |
| 75 | Queen Elizabeth (cruise liner sunk off 837 HKG Hong KonG) |

76	Garden Shed
76	Gas Station
76	Ghost Ship (sea, space)
76	Giedi Prime (oil-surfaced planet in *Dune*)
76	Golden Square, London
76	Grand Prix
76	Ground Zero
76	Jabba's Palace (*Return of the Jedi*)
76	Jewellery Store

77	Girl Guides
77	Global Gathering (worldwide electronic music festivals)
77	*GQ* magazine (Objects appear, perhaps as *a la Fight Club* moving representations, within)

78	Games Room
78	Grand Hotel
78	Grey Havens (Middle-Earth)
78	Guest House
78	Guild Heighliner (*Dune*)

79	GIbraltar
79	GeNesis
79	Jefferson Institute (fictional facility in *Coma* for the preservation of donor bodies, which hang suspended)

80	Hide Out
80	Railway Tunnel
80	Rally Track
80	*Rollerball* (1975/2002) Track
80	Round Table (Camelot)
80	Running Track
80	toRT (breach of civil duty)

81	Hell's Angels
81	Reception Area
81	THAiland (Bangkok)
81	toRA [(Hebrew) the body of Jewish law and learning, including sacred literature and oral tradition]

82	Horizon Line
82	Recycle Bin
82	Re-entry Vehicle
82	Research Vessel

83	Host Computer
83	Hospital Ward
83	Hypersleep Chamber
83	Race Course
83	Residential Care
83	Road Works
83	Roller Coaster
83	Rouge City (*A.I. Artificial Intelligence*)

84	Hair Dresser
84	Helm's Deep, Middle-Earth
84	Help Desk
84	Rail Depot
84	Rep-detect Division (*Blade Runner*)

| 85 | HE (I think of Europa, island in Greek myth defended by the giant man of bronze, Talos) |

85	Home Exhibition
85	Hundred Yards (ten lanes and ten-yard markers makes a 100-Object Location)
85	oRE (mine)
85	Railroad Yard
85	Real Estate
85	Roman Empire
86	High School
86	Homeless Shelter
86	Horse Stables
86	Hyde Park, London
86	Railway Station
86	Rain Forest
86	Red Sea, 575 EGYpt
86	Red Square, 816 RUSsia
86	Retail Park
86	Rivendell Ford, Middle-Earth
87	**HQ**
87	River Gorge
87	Road Junction
88	Hadley's Hope (colony in *Aliens*)
88	Haunted House
88	High Rise
88	Hill House (*The Haunting*)
88	Hillside Railway
88	Hotel Room
88	Reading Room
88	Residence Hall
88	Rest Rooms
88	Rush Hour (heavy traffic area; workplaces being vacated *en masse*)
89	HI HawaIi (Honolulu)
89	Holiday Inn
89	Rekall, Inc. (*Total Recall*)
89	RI Rhode Island (Providence)
89	Rock Island
89	TRInidad and Tobago (port of 566 ESP Spain)
90	Information Technology
90	IO (volcanic moon of Jupiter)
90	Nature Trail
90	New Orleans, 21 LA Louisiana
90	Nuclear Test
90	*TITanic*

91	IA IowA (Des Moines)
91	Indian Ocean
91	Indoor Arena
91	Information Adjustments
91	Internal Affairs
91	National Assembly
92	ILlinois (Springfield)
92	Information Bureau
92	Naval Base
92	Nude Beach
92	NV NeVada (Carson City)
93	Inflatable Castle
93	Inner City
93	Internet Cafe
93	NC North Carolina (Raleigh)
93	NM New Mexico (Santa Fe)
93	Nottingham Castle, England (*Robin Hood*)
94	IDaho (Boise)
94	Interior Decoration
94	IX (machine planet in *Dune* series)
94	ND North Dakota (Bismarck)
94	Notre Dame, Paris
95	Internet Explorer
95	NEbraska (Lincoln)
95	New You (cosmetic surgery in *Logan's Run*)
95	NY New York (Albany)
95	Twin Iron Engine fighter (*Star Wars*)
96	Ice Palace
96	Industrial Space
96	Information Systems
96	Intellectual Property
96	Nakatomi Plaza (setting for *Die Hard*; Fox Plaza, Century City, 21 LA doubled)
96	NetScape
96	Niagara Falls
96	North-South
97	Iwo Jima (volcanic, rather ashen island fought over between the 161 USA and 769 JPN during WW2)
97	Narrow Gauge (railway)
97	NJ New Jersey (Trenton)
97	toNG [(Chinese) a Chinese guild or secret society,

particularly one associated with organized crime]

98	Ice Hockey
98	Information Retrieval (*Brazil*)
98	Inland Revenue, England
98	**NH** New Hampshire (Concord)
98	Nature Reserve
98	Nursing Home

99	**IN**diana (Indianapolis)
99	Tir Na Nog (land of youth in Irish mythology)

100	Area Of Transfer
100	t**ATT** [(to make (anything) by tatting; to work at tatting; tatted edging]

101	Room (*Nineteen Eighty-Four*)
101	t**ATU** [(original, Tahitian spelling of *tattoo)* to mark the skin with indelible pigments]

102	**ATL**antis
102	Armoured Transport Vehicle

10	Commandments
103	Air Traffic Control

104	Aircrew Training Device (flight simulator)
104	Anti-Tank Ditch

105	Angels On Earth
105	T**ATE** Gallery, London

106	Airport Transit System
106	Armoured Transport Police
106	Army Test Site
106	Underground Train Station

107	AntiTank Gun

108	Air Transit Route
108	Air Transportable Hospital
108	t**ATH** [cattle dung; coarse tufted grass that grows where this has fallen; to manure]

109	Area Of Impact

110	th Street, 953 NYC
110	Anglo-Australian Telescope, 116 AUStralia

110   AUT Austria (Vienna)

111   Anti-Aircraft Artillery

112   Armored Attack Vehicle

113   AUM (social interaction and meditation)

114   Advanced Ammunition Depot
114   Area Air Defence
114   AUD (Latin: hear)

115   "Absolutely Adore You" (phrase I say to animals I feel that way about; perhaps picture an animal sanctuary)
115   UAE United Arab Emirates (Abu Dhabi)

116   AAS (plural: rough, cindery lava)
116   AUStralia (Canberra)

117   Aeromedical Aircraft Group
117   AUG (assault rifle)
117   AUGment (to make larger; enlarge in size, number, strength, or extent; increase)

118   AAH (to exclaim in delight)
118   Air-to-Air Receiving/Refuelling

119   Air-to-Air Intercept
119   tUAN [(Malay) sir, lord, master; also, an Australian marsupial, aka wambenger or brush-tailed phascogale]

120   Assembly Line Order

121   ABA (sleeveless garment)
121   ALA [ALighting/Army Launch Area; wing; (Sanskrit: 'hand-clapping') traditional rhythmic pattern in Indian music]
121   tAVA [(Hindi) a griddle in Indian cookery]
121   tUBA
121   ULU (Eskimo knife)

122   ALB (long-sleeved vestment)
122   ALBania (Tirana)
122   ALL
122   tALL

123   ABC (161 USA news network; studios at Times Square, 953 NYC)
123   ALM (river in Upper 110 AUT Austria)

123	Aruba Bonaire Curacao (Dutch islands off the 259 VENezuelan coast)
123	*Pelham*
123	tALC
123	tALK
124	Air Base Defense
124	ALDeraan (*Star Wars*)
124	As-Built Drawings
125	ABE (Lincoln Memorial, 31 WA)
125	ALE
125	InterCity (early 728 GBR 860 High Speed Train)
125	tALE
125	TUBE (the London Subway System)
126	ALP (high mountain)
126	Alpine Bob Sleigh
126	Used Book Shop
127	Air Bursting Grenade
127	Aircraft Landing Gear
127	ALGeria (Algiers)
128	Actual Bodily Harm
128	Advanced Breeder Reactor
129	AirBorNe
129	tABI [(Japanese) a kind of sock worn with Japanese sandals]
129	tALI [(pl.) ankle bones]
130	*A Clockwork Orange*
130	ACT
130	tACO
130	tACT
131	Advanced Cargo Aircraft
131	AKA
131	AMA (Oriental nurse)
131	Upper Memory Area
132	Asphalt-Concrete Base
132	AWL (pointed punching tool)
133	ACCident
133	Advanced Mission Computer
133	Advanced Motion Control
133	Underground City, Montreal, 319 CAN

133	Upper Middle Class (typical residence thereof)

133   Upper Middle Class (typical residence thereof)

134   Advanced Conceptual Design
134   Army Candidate Depot

135   **ACE**
135   **-ACY** [(L; G) state or quality of]
135   Advanced Computing Environment
135   **AWE** (to inspire with ~; Atomic Weapons Establishment)
135   t**AME**

136   **AMP**
136   o**AKS**

137   Air Cargo Glider
137   Amphibious Combat Group

138   **ACR**opolis, 785 GREece
138   Adult Care Home
138   o**UCH**
138   to**UCH**
138   **UKR**aine (Kiev)

139   **AM**bient Intelligence (electronic environment sensitive and responsive to the presence of people, apparently as in Bill Gates' house)
139   t**AKI** [(Mongolian) a rare wild horse]

140   **ADO** (bustle)
140   Arc De Triomphe, 681 FRA
140   **UDO** (Japanese herb)

141   Air Defense Area/Artillery

142   **AXL**

143   Adult Day Care
143   Air Defense Command

144   **ADD**
144   **ADD**ress
144   Advanced Dungeons and Dragons
144   Air Defense District

145   AirDrop Equipment
145   **AXE**

146   **ADS** (**AD**vertisement**S**)

| 146 | **ADZ** (cutting tool) |

147   **A**ir **D**efence **G**round (environment: the network of ground radar sites and command and control centres within a specific theater of operations which are used for the tactical control of air defence operations)/**G**un

147   **A**irfield **D**efense **G**uard

148   **ADH**esive (perhaps picture **O**bjects on top of vast sheet of flypaper)

148   **A**ir **D**efence **R**adar/**R**egion

148   **A**ircraft **D**amage **R**epair

148   **A**lcoholic and **D**rug **R**ecovery

149   **A**ir **D**efence **I**ntercept

149   **A**ltitude **D**isplay **I**ndicator

149   t**AXI**

150   **A**fter **E**xtra **T**ime (perhaps picture a soccer penalty shootout with players taking turns from the center circle)

150   **A**rmy **E**xtension **T**raining

151   **A**rea **51** (military testing base), 92 NV

151   **A**uto**E**rotic **A**sphyxiation

152   **A**ft **E**quipment **B**ay

152   **A**uxiliary **E**quipment **B**uilding

152   t**AEL** [(Malay) a denomination of money, also, a weight of one ounce and one-third]

153   **A**rchitecture, **E**ngineering and **C**onstruction

153   **A**rea **E**quipment **C**ompound

153   **A**rmy **E**ducation/**E**valuation **C**entre

154   **A**ctive **E**lectronic **D**ecoy

154   **A**erobic **E**xercise

155   **A**dult **E**ntertainment **E**xpo

155   **A**dverse **E**nvironmental **E**ffect

155   **AYE** (affirmative vote)

156   **A**ir **E**quipment and **S**upport

156   **A**ll-**E**lectric **S**hip

157   **AEG**ean sea (between 785 GREece and 18 TURkey)

157   **A**ir **E**xpeditionary **G**roup

157   **A**ircraft **E**valuation **G**roup

158	**AER** [(Latin) 198 AIR]
158	Antenna Effective Height
158	Army Emergency Relief

| 159 | Unit Effectiveness Inspection |

160	Advanced Passenger Train
160	o**UZO** (aniseed-flavoured Greek liqueur)
160	to**AST**
160	**UFO**

161	**ASA** American Samoa [Pago Pago (de facto); Fagatogo (seat of government)]
161	t**UFA** [(Ital.) a rock made of fine volcanic detritus]
161	**USA** (Washington, DC)

162	Alaska Pipeline Bridge
162	All Points Bulletin
162	Armoured Fighting Vehicle
162	**UZB**ekistan (Tashkent)

163	After School Club
163	Amateur Swimming Club
163	**ASK**
163	t**ASK** (Force)
163	t**USK**

| 164 | After School Detention |
| 164 | Airport Surface Detection |

165	**APE**
165	**ASY**lum
165	**AZE**rbaijan (Baku)
165	t**APE**

166	Animal Swimming Pool
166	**APP**lication (computer program)
166	**ASP**
166	**ASS**
166	T**AFF** Island, Wales
166	T**ASS** (186 URS Soviet Union news agency)
166	t**UFF** (a general term for all consolidated pyroclastic rock)

| 167 | **AFG**hanistan (Kabul) |

168	**ASH**
168	t**ASH** [(Scots) to soil, blemish]
168	t**USH**

169	United States Navy
169	**UZI**

170	Above Ground Test
170	Advanced Jet Trainer
170	**AGO** (in the past)
170	UnderGround Test

171	**AGA** (Turkish military officer)
171	**UGA**nda (Kampala)
171	Urban Growth Area

172	Above Ground Level
172	Aerodrome Ground Lighting
172	Air to Ground Laser

173	**AGro**Chemicals
173	**Air-to-Ground** Missile
173	Annual General Meeting

174	**AGree**D
174	ADS-B **Guidance Display** (aircraft computer display of Location)

175	**AGE**
175	-**AGE** [(L) action or state of]
175	**AGE**ncy
175	Army Ground Equipment

176	Advanced Graphics Processor
176	Airborne Ground Surveillance
176	Anti-**G**ravity Suit (floating over Objects)
176	Army General Staff

177	**AGG**ravated (weather-worn Objects)
177	**AGG**regate (the deciding match in an aggregate fixture)
177	**AGG**ro
177	Under-**G**ravel Jets (aquarium; maybe picture a huge one to accommodate all the Objects)

178	Advanced-**G**as Cooled Reactor
178	**AGH**!
178	to**UGH**
178	**UGH**!
178	Under Ground Hotel

179	Above Ground Installation

179	Active Galactic Nucleus
179	**AG**ai**N** (amateur radio)
179	**AGI**lity (an athlete agilely negotiating all the Objects in this Location)
179	Upper Gastro-Intestinal

180	**ART**
180	**AHO** Netherlands Antilles (Willemstad)
180'	(skateboard bowl)
180	t**ART**

181	**A-HA**
181	Aerial Rocket Artillery
181	Arrived Holding Area
181	**ARU**ba (Oranjestad)
181	Australian Regular Army
181	t**ARA** [(Maori) a variety of bracken found in 962 New ZeaLand and 116 AUS Tasmania]
181	**URU**guay (Montevideo)

182	**ARB** (**BA**ttle Damage **R**epair Ship; an incongruous acronym)
182	**URB**an area
182	**URL** (another word for a Net address/the full path to any given web page or graphic on the Internet: http://www.example.com)

183	**ARC** (to travel a curved course)
183	**ARC**ade
183	**ARK**
183	**ARM** (probably in front of you)
183	**ARM**enia (Yerevan)

184	After Hours Depository
184	**AH**ea**D**
184	Auxiliary Repair Dry Dock

185	Aircraft Recovery Equipment
185	Alert Readiness Exercise
185	**ARE**
185	-**ARY** [(L) place for, dealing with]
185	t**ARE** (a leg and groin protector used in a number of Japanese martial arts; Japanese dipping sauce)

186	Animal Rescue Site
186	**ARS** Salvage Ship classification
186	t**URF**

187	Air Refuelling Group
187	Air Rescue Group
187	ARGentina (Buenos Aires)
188	**AHH**
188	13 AK AlasKa RailRoad
188	Armed Reconnaissance Helicopter
188	**ARR**angement
188	**ARR**ival
188	Attack Helicopter Regiment
188	t**AHR** (a Himalayan wild goat)
189	**AHI** (tuna)
189	t**ARN** (a lake in the bedrock basin of a cirque)
189	t**URN**
189	**URN**
190	**AIT** (small island)
190	**ANT**
190	**ANT**arctica
190	**ANT**igua and Barbuda (Saint John's)
191	Adult Image Archive
191	167 AFGhan National Army
191	Air force/Navy/Army
191	t**ANA** [(Hindi) an Indian police station]
191	t**UNA**
192	**AIL**
192	All Night Long (party)
192	A Net Laying Ship
192	t**AIL**
193	African National Congress
193	**ANC**ient
193	t**ANK**
194	Alpha Numeric Display
194	**AID**
194	**AND**
194	**AND**orra (Andorra la Vella)
195	**ANY**
195	Asia and Near East
195	t**UNE**
195	Underground Nuclear Explosion
195	User Interface Environment

196	**AIS** (three-toed sloth)
196	**A**ll-**N**ight **P**arty
196	**A**utonomic **N**ervous **S**ystem
196	**'UNS** (ones; maybe picture all Objects here in plural, reflected in one or more mirrors as other *a la The Matrix Reloaded* multiple embodiments or representations?)

197	**A**ir **N**ational **G**uard, 161 USA
197	**ANG**le (perhaps picture all Objects here inside an outsize angle sign)
197	**ANG**ola (Luanda)
197	t**ANG**
197	t**UNG** (a kind of Chinese tree)

198	**AIR** (see also 158 AER)
198	**A**rtificial **N**utrition and **H**ydration

199	**A**rmy **IN**stallation
199	**ANI** (tropical American black cuckoo)
199	**ANI**mation
199	t**AIN** (paper-thin tin plate; tin foil used as a backing for mirrors)

200	**BOT**
200	**BOT**swana (Gaborone)
200	**BT** **T**ower, London (restaurant on top floor)
200	**LOO**
200	**LOT**

201	**B**ank **O**f **A**merica
201	**BOA**
201	**L**ime **T**ree **A**venue, England
201	**L**oss **O**f **A**ircraft (a crash site)
201	**LTU** **L**i**Th****U**ania (Vilnius)

202	**BOB**
202	**BOL**ivia (Sucre: constitutional capital; La Paz: seat of government)
202	**LOB**
202	o**BOL** [(Greek) a Greek coin]

203	**BOW** (a ship's front)
203	**B**asic **T**raining **C**entre
203	**B**usiness **T**raining **C**entre
203	**LOC** [(Latin) place; speak]
203	**LOW**

204	**B**oard **O**f **D**irectors

204	**BOX**
204	**LOX** (Liquid **OX**ygen)

205	**BOY**
205	o**BOE** (a double-reed treble woodwind instrument)
205	**VOE** (small inlet, creek or bay)

206   **BOP** (or be**BOP**: style of jazz developed in the early and mid-1940s characterized by fast tempo, instrumental virtuosity and improvisation based on the combination of harmonic structure and melody)

206	**BOZ**
206	Lake **Of** **F**ire
206	Line **Of** **S**ight
206	**LOP**

207	**BOG**
207	**LOG**

208   **B**efore **O**ffice **H**ours (picture empty or under-populated office in dimmer lighting)

208   **BOR**ough

208   Left-To-Right (6 Supermarket content generally so ordered in the West to match our educated perceptual sweep; the opposite in the Orient. Objects - perhaps simultaneously - flopped or rotated on their horizontal perceptual axis)

209   **BON** [Japanese Buddhist custom to honour the departed (deceased) spirits of one's ancestors. This Buddhist custom has evolved into a family reunion holiday during which people return to ancestral family places and visit and clean their ancestors' graves, and when the spirits of ancestors are supposed to revisit the household altars]

209   **Ba**T**talio**N (military unit of around 300–1,300 soldiers usually consisting of between two and seven companies and typically commanded by either a Lieutenant Colonel or a Colonel. Several battalions are grouped to form a regiment or a brigade)

209   All **LON**don airports code

209   **L**ost **T**ime **I**ncident (e.g. a 160 UFO abduction)

210	**BAT**
210	**BUT** (flatfish)
210	**LAO**s (Vientiane)
210	**LAT**via (Riga)
210	**VAT**

211	**BAA** (to bleat; a sheep field)

211	**B**omber **A**lert **A**rea
211	**B**uilt-**U**p **A**rea
212	**B**ed **A**nd **B**reakfast
212	**BUL**garia (Sofia)
212	**LAB**oratory
212	o**VAL**
213	**BUM**
213	**LAC** (French for *lake*; resinous substance secreted by insects)
213	**LAM** (in flight, esp. from the law)
213	**LAW** (to sue)
213	**LUC** [(Latin) light]
213	**LUM** (chimney)
213	o**VUM** (female reproductive cell)
214	**BAD**
214	**BUD** (small protuberance on a branch or stem; -weiser: perhaps picture the manufacturing plant)
214	**LAD**
214	**LAX** (21 LA International Airport)
214	**L**ife **A**fter **D**eath (supernatural events - séances, poltergeist activity with the Objects being tossed around etc.)
214	**L**ight **A**rmored **D**ivision
214	**LUX**embourg (Luxembourg)
215	**BAY** (to howl; docking)
215	**LAY** [(of the land) nature or topography of the surrounding landscape]
215	**VUE** [(French feminine adjective) seen; 728 GBR cinema chain]
216	**BAP**
216	**BUS** (in computer architecture, a subsystem that transfers data between components inside a or between computers)
216	**LAP** (Objects around a Buddha statue or in a spotlight on your lap)
217	**BAG** (-gage: as in airport carousel)
217	**BUG**
217	**LAG**
217	**LUG**
217	Room (*The Shining* novel and TV series)
218	**BAH**amas (Nassau)
218	**BAR**

218	BARbados (Bridgetown)
218	BURkina Faso (Ouagadougou)

219	BAN
219	BANgladesh (Dhaka)
219	BUN
219	Light Armoured Infantry
219	Local Area Network (network created with cables that connects computers located within a small area such as an office)
219	VAN [Vein Artery Nerve important structures in the costal - 892 RIB - groove (in order going interiorly)]
219	VANuatu (Port Vila)

220	Large Binocular Telescope, 16 AZ
220	Low Level Trajectory
220	Low Lunar Orbit
220	Volcano Lava Tube

221	Latitude, Longitude, Altitude
221	LBA LiByA (Tripoli)
221	Low Level Airspace (below 18 000 feet ASL)

222	Billion BarreLs (usually in reference to oil production)
222	Bunker Busting Bomb (Objects in the area of a many-storied bunker being busted)
222	B2B (Business-2-Business: business transactions between, for example, a manufacturer and a wholesaler or a wholesaler and a retailer)
222	LLB [undergraduate, or bachelor, degree in law (or a first professional degree in law, depending on jurisdiction) originating in England and offered in most common law countries as the primary law degree. The LLB was established as a liberal arts degree, which requires that the student undertake a certain amount of study of the classics]

223	BBC (Television Centre, London)
223	Launch Base Complex

224	BLooD (whole Location splattered with it or spraying from a fountain in part of it)
224	Last Line of Defence

225	Bachelor of Business Education (a business school or its students' graduation)
225	Best Before End (stacks of discarded supermarket food)
225	Best BuY (this book and the Objects emerging from within)
225	BLY

225	Location Based Entertainment (a live outside broadcast)

226	BarreLS
226	Local Bike Shop
226	Lunar Landing Simulator
226	Very Low Frequency [radio frequencies (RF) in the range of 3 kHz to 30 kHz. Since there is not much bandwidth in this band of the radio spectrum, only the very simplest signals, such as for radio navigation are used]

227	BBQ

228	BLR BeLaRus (Minsk)
228	Broken Beyond Repair
228	Burnt Beyond Repair
228	LBR LiBeRia (Monrovia)

229	BaLlooN
229	Battleground Light Infantry
229	BlockBuster, Inc. (digital rental store)

230	Basic Combat Training
230	LooKouT

231	Launch Control Area (usually with reference to missiles)
231	LCA Saint LuCiA (Castries)
231	Light Combat Aircraft

232	LoCaL
232	Lunar Cargo Lander

233	BackCountry Cooking (in the wild)
233	Launch Control Centre
233	Lower Middle Class (typical residence thereof)

234	Blue Compact Dwarf (galaxy)
234	BMX (course)
234	Bridge of Khazad-Dum, Middle-Earth
234	Liquid Crystal Display (a type of flat-panel display for TVs and computer monitors)

235	Before the Common Era (non-religious alternative to the use of 23 BC in designating the first period of the Gregorian Calendar, the era of prehistory and much of antiquity)
235	Life Changing Event

236	BarracKS
236	LaKeS

236	Vatican City State
236	VCS Atari

237	BacKGround
237	Brightest Cluster Galaxy
237	Room [*The Shining* (1980)]

238	BaKeR
238	BeaCH
238	Large Conference Room
238	LaunCH
238	LWH (volume of a rectangular solid)

239	BroKeN (aviation - very cloudy)
239	Brain-Computer Interface (direct communication pathway between a brain and an external device. BCIs are often aimed at assisting, augmenting or repairing human cognitive or sensory- motor functions)
239	Landing Craft, Infantry
239	La Cosa Nostra (the Mafia)

240	British Dependent Territories
240	Brittle-Ductile Transition (strongest part of the Earth's crust)
240	Light Diesel Oil (petroleum)
240	Light Duty Truck

241	Blast Danger Area
241	Bomb Damage Assessment
241	Bomb Disposal Unit
241	Business Development Unit
241	Labour and Delivery Unit
241	Low Density Area

243	Blood Donor Centre

244	Large Digit Display (for e.g. large 1 Airport or 86 Railway Station arrivals/departures)
244	Loss, Damage or Destruction (e.g. post-rioting scene)

245	Best Day Ever
245	BounDarY
245	oLDY [(coll.) an old person or thing]

246	BorDer Check/Crossing Point

247	BuilDinG
247	LanDinG
247	LoDGe

248	Battle Damage Repair
248	BorDeR

249	BDI BurunDI (Bujumbura)
249	LonDoN, England

250	BET
250	BEThlehem, 968 ISRael
250	LET
250	oLEO [(abbr. *oleograph*) a lithographic repro of an oil painting]
250	VET

251	Building Evacuation Area
251	LEA (meadow)

252	B-52 bomber
252	Behind Enemy Lines
252	BELgium (Brussels)
252	BEL

253	BECk (mountain stream)
253	*Blue Electric Chair* (Warhol print)
25C	(amusement arcade or Location awash with quarters)

254	BED (shaking, spinning, river, sea etc.)
254	LED (semiconductor light source used as indicator lamps in many devices and increasingly so for lighting. Introduced as a practical electronic component in 1962, early 254 LEDs emitted low-intensity red light, but modern versions are available across the visible, ultraviolet and infrared wavelengths, with very high brightness. Perhaps visualise entire Location partially illuminated by them)
254	LEX [(Latin) law]
254	oLED (organic Light Emitting Diode): LED in which the emissive electroluminescent layer is a film of organic compounds that emits light when an electric current passes through it. This layer of organic semiconductor material is formed between two electrodes. Generally, at least one of these electrodes is transparent)

255	BEE
255	BYE
255	LEE (shelter from the wind)
255	LEY (pasture: a field covered with grass or herbage and suitable for grazing by livestock)
255	LYE (solution used to make soap)

256	**BE**havioral Science
256	**BYP**ass
256	**LES**bos, 785 GREece
256	**LES**otho (Maseru)
256	Lower East Side, Manhattan
257	**BEG**
257	**LEG** (one of usually two-match sports tie)
257	**VEG** (-etation)
258	**BER**muda (Hamilton) (also: the Triangle)
258	Local Electricity Room
258	Local Equipment Room
258	o**VER** (to go, leap or vault over)
259	**BEN** (inner room)
259	**BEN**in (Porto-Novo)
259	o**VEN**
259	**VEN**ezuela (Caracas)
260	Base Supply Office
260	Basic Survival Training (usually in the wild)
260	Building Pressure Testing (increasing vibrations cause certain Objects to shift, topple, collide, break etc.)
260	Lost Property Office
260	2nd Street Tunnel (location in *Blade Runner*), 21 LA
261	Basic Service Area (stop for refreshment, relief, shopping and refuelling on major road)
261	Beach Support Area
261	Blood Supply Unit
261	Learning Support Unit
261	Visual Processing Unit (specialized microprocessor that offloads and accelerates 3D or 2D graphics rendering from the microprocessor; Objects represented by)
262	Below Sea Level
262	**B**irth**PL**ace
263	Battle Simulation Centre
263	Big Sur, 31 CA
263	**BSc**
263	Life Sciences Centre
263	Local SuperCluster (galaxies)
264	Beach Party Division
264	Large Screen Display

| 276 | BattleGrouP (usually a fleet of warships) |
| 276 | Below Ground Surface |

277	Big Green Gathering (annual festival, 728 GBR)
277	281 BRAzilian Jiu-Jitsu
277	Local Group of Galaxies [comprises more than 30 galaxies (including dwarf galaxies), with its gravitational centre located somewhere between our galaxy, the Milky Way and the Andromeda Galaxy]

278	Bill Gates' House
278	Big Game Hunters
278	Little Girls' Room
278	Low Glass House

| 279 | Video Gamer Network |

280	BHOpal, 994 INDia
280	BRO
280	Left Hand Traffic
280	Light Rapid Transit
280	Lunar Reconnaissance/Robotic Orbiter

281	BHUtan (Thimphu)
281	BRA (gigantic one enveloping Objects)
281	BRAzil (Brasilia)
281	BRUnei (Bandar Segi Begawan)

| 282 | Big Red Button (initiating nuclear attack: Objects blown over and apart at a distance from explosion) |
| 282 | Long Range Laser |

283	BReaK (30 MO)
283	BRooK
283	Language Resource Centre

284	BeachHeaD
284	Blue Ray Disc (picture Objects played thereupon)
284	BRoaDcast (outside, live etc.)

| 285 | Bulk HYdrogen (balloon) |
| 285 | Least Restrictive Environment (nude, free-fall, solitude etc.) |

286	Local Hobby Store
286	Long Range Patrol
286	VHF (radio frequency range from 30 MHz to 300 MHz)

286   VHS

287   **BR**id**G**e
287   Long **R**an**G**e aircraft (aircraft such as Stealth)

288   **BRR!** (freezing environment)
288   *Little Red Riding Hood*

289   **B**a**H**rai**N** (Manama)
289   Long **R**ange **I**nterceptor (high speed launch vessel with rigid inflatable hull designed deployed from cutters via a rear launching ramp)
289   Low **R**esolution **I**mage (Objects seen thus)

290   **BIT** [(**BI**nary Digi**T**) a 1 or 0 used as the basic unit of digital storage; to restrain with a **BIT**]
290   o**BIT** [(Lat.) a religious office for a dead person]
290   **BIO** (life; Objects as living, moving things a la *Sorcerer's Apprentice* as living, moving things)
290   **LIT** [light; former Lithuanian monetary unit (litas)]
290   o**LIO** (a savoury dish of meat and vegetable)

291   **VIA** (by way of; -duct)

292   **BIB** (to drink alcohol: think of a party)
292   **LIB** Lebanon (Beirut)
292   **LIB**eration

293   **BIC**
293   **VIC**arage
293   **VIC**tory (celebrations)
293   **VIM** (energy)

294   **BID**
294   **LID**
294   **ln x** (Natural log)
294   o**LID** (rank-smelling)
294   **VID**eo

295   **LIE**
295   **LIE**chtenstein (Vaduz)
295   **VIE**tnam (Hanoi)

296   **BIZ** Bel**IZ**e (formerly British Honduras)
296   **BIS** (**BI**sexual**S**)
296   **BIZ**
296   Line **I**n the **S**and
296   **LIP** (to cheek)

| 296 | **VIP** |
| 296 | **VIS** (force or power; see) |

297	**BIG**
297	**LIG** [(esp. in the entertainment industry and media) a function at which free entertainment and refreshments are available; to attend such a function in order to take advantage of free entertainment and refreshments; freeload]
297	**VIG** [charge paid to a bookie on a bet (vigorish)]

| 298 | **BIH** Bosnia and Herzegovina (Sarajevo) |

299	**BIN** (Objects as discarded or recyclable in outsize such)
299	**LIN** (waterfall; Objects in cave network behind)
299	**VIN** Saint Vincent and the Grenadines (Kingstown)

300	**COO**
300	**COT**
300	Crew Transfer Tunnel
300	Ministry Of True (Minitrue; *Nineteen Eighty-Four)*
300	**MOO**
300	**WOT**

301	Court Of Appeal
301	Karate Training Academy
301	**KOA** (timber tree)
301	**MOA** (extinct flightless bird)

302	**COB**
302	**COL** [(Latin) together]
302	**COL**ombia (Bogota)
302	**COL**osseum
302	**KOB** (reddish brown antelope)
302	**MOB** (e.g. Mafia)
302	**MOL** [Ministry Of Love (MiniLove) in *Nineteen Eighty-Four*; unit of quantity in chemistry (mole)]

303	Canals Of Mars
303	**COK CO**o**K** Islands (Avarua)
303	**COM**oros (Moroni)
303	**COW**
303	**MOC** (-casin)
303	**MOW**
303	**WOK**
303	**WOW**

304	City **O**f **D**omes (*Logan's Run*)
304	**COD**
304	**COD** Democratic Republic of the Congo (Kinshasa)
304	**COX**
304	**MOD**
304	**W**all **O**f **D**eath
305	**C**i**TY**
305	**CO**mpan**Y**
305	**C**ouncil **O**f **E**lrond, Middle-Earth
305	**C**oun**TY**
305	**COY**
305	**WOE** (tremendous grief)
306	**COP**
306	**C**orridors **O**f **P**ower
306	**COS** (lettuce; think of a lettuce field)
306	**COS**ine
306	**KOP** (colloquial name or term for a number of terraces and stands at sports stadiums, particularly in 728 GBR Great Britain, so named due to their steep nature, resembling a hill near Ladysmith 861 RSA South Africa that was the scene of the Battle of Spion Kop during the Second Boer War)
306	**M**inistry **O**f **S**ound, London and dance compilations
306	**MOP** (Location floor being mopped)
306	**MOZ**ambique (Maputo)
306	**W**ell **O**f **S**ouls (*Raiders Of The Lost Ark*)
307	**C**hurch **O**f **G**od
307	**COG**
307	**M**ee**T**in**G**
307	**MOG** (to move away)
307	**W**alls **O**f **J**ericho
308	**COR** [(Latin) heart]
308	**COR**oner
308	**KOR** South **KOR**ea (Seoul) (683 PRK North Korea)
308	**MOR** (forest humus)
309	**CON** [(Latin) with]
309	**CON**voy
309	**KOI** (large Japanese carp)
309	**M**inistry **O**f **I**nformation (London; *Brazil*)
309	**MON** (man)
309	**MON**aco (Monaco)
309	**MTN** **M**auri**T**a**N**ia (Nouakchott)

310	**CAT** (to anchor to a **CAT**head: large wooden beam located on either bow of a sailing ship, and angled outward at roughly 45')
310	**CAT**astrophe
310	**CAT**hedral
310	**C**ombat **A**ir **O**perations
310	**CUT**
310	**KAT** (evergreen shrub; also: 710 Q**AT**)
310	**MAT**
310	**MUT** (ancient Egyptian mother goddess)
311	**C**entral **A**ccumulation **A**rea (hazardous waste management)
311	**C**entral **A**rid **A**sia
311	**C**ontrolled **A**ccess **A**rea
312	**CAB**
312	**C**itizen's **A**dvice **B**ureau
312	**C**rash **A**nd **B**urn
312	**CUB**
312	**CUB**a (Havana)
313	**CAM**
313	**CAM**pus
313	**CAM**bodia (Phnom Penh)
313	**CAW**
313	**CUM**
313	**KUW**ait (Kuwait City)
313	**MAC**
313	**MAW** **MA**la**Wi** (Lilongwi)
313	**MUM** (to act in disguise)
314	**CAD**
314	**C**omputer-**A**ided **D**esign (graphics programs for designing such 3D objects as cars, buildings and bridges)
314	**CUD** (food portion to be chewed again)
314	**MAD**
314	**MAD**agascar (Antananarivo)
314	**MUD**
314	**WAD**
314	**WAX**
315	**CAY** (small low island)
315	**CAY**man Islands (George Town)
315	**C**eti **A**lpha **5** (windswept barren planet in *Star Trek II*)
315	**C**omputer-**A**ided **E**ngineering
315	**CUE**

316	CAF Central African Republic (Bangui)
316	CAP (take; head)
316	CUP
316	KAS (large cupboard/plural of ka)
316	KAZakhstan (Astana)
316	MAP
316	Marks And Spencer
316	MAS MAlaySia (Kuala Lumpur)
317	KAG
317	MAG
317	MUG
317	WAG
318	CAR
318	CARousel
318	CUR (mongrel)
318	MAR
318	MAR Morocco (Rabat)
318	WAR
319	CAN
319	CANada (Ottawa)
319	MAN [(Latin) hand]
320	ComBaT
320	Chemical and Biological Terrorism
320	Combined Bomber Offensive
320	Computer-Based Training
320	MLT MaLTa [Valletta (*de facto*)]
320	Web-Based Training
321	Central Business Area
321	Close Battle Area (melee or siege)
321	oMBU [(Guarani) a S.American tree, that grows in the pampas]
322	*Celebrity Big Brother*
322	CLuB
322	College BasketBall
322	Men's BasketBall
323	CaLM
323	CLoCk (public one, like Big Ben, London)
323	Crew Briefing Centre
323	MiLK (Objects splashed with)
323	Mountain Bike Club

324	Central Business District
324	CLouD (descending upon Location)
32X	Sega

325	-CLE [(L) diminutive]
325	Cross Bronx Expressway
325	Motor Boat and Yachting

326	Campus Bus Service
326	CBS
326	CLaSS
326	CLoSe (an enclosure; land held as private property)
326	oWLS

327	Carrier Battle Group
327	CoLleGe
327	Wing Landing Gear (perhaps skimming, blowing or knocking aside Objects during landing)

328	CLeaR (transparent Objects)
328	CLeaRing (forest)
328	Coal/Coke Bulk Handling (from mine surface to such transport as a train)

329	China-Burma-India (WWII theater of war)
329	CLeaN (all Objects thus)
329	CLInic
329	Mig-29
329	MLI MaLI (Bamako)

| 330 | CirCuiT (dirt-bike, model train etc.) |
| 330 | Cu Chi Tunnels (underground living and ambush network), 295 VIEtnam |

331	Mig-31 (also fictional name for *Firefox)*
331	Mixed Martial Arts
331	MotorCycle Accident (knocking Objects over)

332	Median Water Level (water perhaps halfway up average-sized Object)
332	MiCroLight (circling the Objects)
332	Windows Media Video (video and audio of Objects within)

333	Child Care Centre
333	CWM [(Welsh) circular basin with steep walls (cirque)]
333	Working Men's Club
333	World Wide Web

334	Coal Mine Drainage (picture the connecting tunnels and Objects being drained of a minor flood)
334	MCD
334	MKD MaCeDonia (Skopje)

335	all over the OCCY (in every direction; an explosion or a dispersal)

336	ChecKPoint

337	Cartesian Coordinate Grid
337	Kids With Guns
337	Match-Winning Goal
337	Walk With Jesus

338	Central Control Room
338	CMR CaMeRoon (Yaounde)
338	Main Conference Room

339	CoMmoN (piece of open land for public use, especially in a village or 39 toWN)
339	Man Machine Interface (gateway to inner world of *Tron*)

340	Medical Doctor's Office

341	Cote D'Azur (681 FRA French Riviera)
341	Crash-Damaged Aircraft
341	MDA MolDovA (Chisinau)

342	MoDuLe
342	MDV MalDiVes (Male)

343	Cash Deposit Machine
343	Central Distribution Centre (Amazon)
343	MeaDoW

344	Mine Detection Dog (sniffing each Object in turn)

345	Career Development Event
345	Common Desktop Environment

346	Cul De Sac
346	Main Distribution Frame

347	Cave Diving Group
347	Charles De Gaulle (statue and code for airport of several concentric levels)
347	Military Data Gathering

348	CD-Recordable/Recorder
348	Competition Dirt Riders
348	Crash Damage Repair
348	Main Distribution Room (electricity, telephony etc.)
349	Community Day Nursery
350	MET (-tropolis; -tropolitan)
350	WET
351	Central Electronics Assembly
351	KEA (New Zealand parrot)
351	Marine Expeditionary Unit
351	Mise En Abyme
351	MYAnmar/Burma (Naypyidaw)
351	Wind Energy Area
352	CEL (drawn frame of animation)
352	WEB
352	MEL (honey)
353	Career Ending Move
353	CEMetery
353	CYClone
353	KEW
353	Mars Excursion Module
353	Mars Expeditionary Complex
353	MEM (Hebrew letter)
353	MEW
353	MYC (any of a group of vertebrate oncogenes whose product, a DNA binding protein, is thought to promote the growth of tumor cells)
354	KEX (dry, hollow stalk)
354	MED
354	MEXico (City)
354	WED
355	KEY
355	Know Your Enemy (Objects used in turn as target practice)
355	tWEE (affectedly cute or quaint)
355	WEE
355	WYE [a support or other structure shaped in particular like a Y; a triangle of railroad track, used for turning locomotives or trains; (in plumbing) a short pipe with a branch joining it at an acute angle]

356	CEP (large mushroom - a cloud)
356	Consumer Electronics Show
356	CYPrus (Nicosia)
356	KEF (marijuana)
356	KEP (to catch)
356	oWES [(3rd.) OWE; to be in debt for]

357	Convoy Escort Group (Group's weapons playing over each Object in turn)
357	CYGnus (swan-shaped constellation)
357	KEG (small barrel)
357	MEG(-abyte)

358	Central Equipment Room
358	Climb En Route
358	Main Engine Room
358	Mars Exploration Rover
358	MER ([French] sea)
358	MERchant
358	oKEH (expressing approval)
358	oMER [(Hebrew) a Hebrew dry measure, = 1/10 EPHA]

359	KEN (to know)
359	KENya (Nairobi)
359	MEN
359	oMEN (to portend)
359	toKEN
359	WEN (benign skin tumor)
359	WYN (rune for 'W')

360	Client/Customer Services Office
360	Confined Space Training
360	Convulsive Shock Therapy
360'	(basketball spin; circling camera full turn; 304 Wall Of Death)

361	Central Processing Unit: the main microprocessor in a computer
361	KSA Kingdom of Saudi Arabia (Riyadh)
361	Maritime Patrol Aircraft
361	Missile Storage Area
361	Water Purification Unit
361	Waste Storage Unit

362	Campus Services Building
362	Coastal/Motor Patrol Boat
362	Computer Science Building
362	CPV CaPe Verde (Praia)

363	Centre for Public Works
363	KFC
363	Men Seeking Women
363	MP3 (files music compressed for but playback still of digital quality)
363	MSc
363	MusculoSKeletal (as footing or loose covering)
363	Women Seeking Men
364	Central Police Department
364	ComPounD
364	Customer Support Desk
364	Manufacturing, Supply and Distribution
364	MP4
365	CaPE
365	CZEch Republic (Prague)
365	MaZE
365	MultiPhase Extraction
365	oWSE [(Scots) an ox]
366	Central/City Police Station
366	Customer Self-Service
366	MaSS
366	MeSS (hall)
367	Coal Seam Gas
368	Centre for Space Research
368	Combat Support Helicopter/Hospital (*M*A*S*H*)
369	Coastal and Small Islands
369	Coral Sea Islands
369	Crash Scene Investigation
369	Crime Scene Investigation
369	MFI (728 GBR large furniture stores chain)
369	MiSsioN
370	CarGO
370	CGO ConGO (Kinshasa)
372	KGB
372	MGL MonGoLia (Ulan Bator)
372	Museums, Galleries, Libraries
373	MGM

374	Cloud-to-Ground Discharge (lightning)
375	CarriaGE
376	Coast Guard Station
376	KGZ KyrGyZstan (Bishkek)
377	Ministero di Grazia e Giustizia (901 ITAlian initialism of the: Ministry of Justice)
378	Computer-Generated Hologram
378	ManaGeR (office and large overlooked workplace)
379	Computer Generated Imagery
379	CorruGated Iron
380	Central Reservation Office
380	CROatia (Zagreb)
380	Cathode Ray Tube (the technology used to create conventional TV's and computer monitors has been largely replaced by 660 FST's)
380	MHO (unit of electrical conductance)
380	WHO
381	CHAd (N'Djamena)
381	Commercial Retail Unit
381	CRU (French wine classification)
381	oKRA (a tropical plant of the mallow family, with edible pods, aka *gumbo*)
381	WHA? (expression of disbelief)
382	Career Resource Library
382	MHL MarsHaLl Islands [Majuro (Delap)]
383	CiRCle
383	CRC Costa RiCa (San Jose)
383	Crowd Riot Control
385	Commercial Real Estate
385	CRY
385	oCHE (the throwing line in darts)
385	WHY (reason or cause of something)
385	WRY
386	CouRSe
386	kiloHertZ
386	MegaHertz: measurement of computer speed in handling data

386	WHSmith
387	CHarGe, CHanGe
389	CHIle (Santiago de 389 CHIle)
389	CHN CHiNa (Beijing)
389	Magnetic Resonance Imaging
389	MRI MauRItius (Port Louis)
390	CouNTry (-side)
390	KIT
390	oMIT
390	tWIT
390	WIT
391	CIA
392	CIV Cote d'IVoire (Yamoussoukro)
392	Men In Black
392	MIB (to play marble)
392	MIL (unit of length)
393	MIM (primly demure)
393	WIM (file: contains 1 or more images in the native Windows Imaging forMat)
394	KID
394	MID (-dle)
394	MIX
395	Continuous Noise Environment (vehicle production line)
395	MNE MoNtEnegro (Podgorica)
396	Central Nursing Station
396	City In Space
396	CommunicatioNS
396	KIF (marijuana)
396	KIP
396	oWNS
396	WIZ
397	MIG (playing marble)
397	tWIG
397	WIG
398	CIRcumference
398	KIR (alcoholic beverage)
398	KIRibati (Tarawa)

398	**MIR** (Russian peasant commune; name of space station)
399	**KIN**
399	o**MNI** (all)
399	t**WIN**
399	**WIN** (to winnow)
400	**DOT**
401	**D**ead **O**n **A**rrival
401	**D**epartment **O**f **A**ccounts/**A**dministration
402	**DOL** (unit of pain intensity)
403	**D**eck **O**f **C**ards
403	**D**epartment **O**f **C**orrections
403	**DOC**
403	**DOM**inican Republic (Santo Domingo)
404	**D**epartment **O**f **D**efense (the Pentagon, 161 USA)
404	**D**irection **O**f **D**eparture
405	**DOE** (female deer)
405	Freeway (major north-south Interstate Highway in Southern 31 CA)
406	**D**epartment **O**f **S**tate
406	**D**epartment **O**f **S**urgery
406	**D**esk**T**op **P**ublishing
407	**D**elay **O**f **G**ratification
407	**D**epartment **O**f **J**ustice, 161 USA
407	**DOG**
408	**D**epartment **O**f **R**ecords
408	*Dukes Of Hazzard*
408	o**DOR** (pervading the Location)
409	**D**epartment **O**f **T**he **N**avy
409	**DON**
410	**D**igital **A**udio **T**ape
410	**DUO** (419 DUI)
411	**D**ense **U**rban **A**rea
411	**D**rug **A**ddiction/**A**lcoholism
412	**DAL** (lentil dish)

412	**D**ead **A**nd **B**uried (cemetery and church)
412	**D**igital **A**udio **B**roadcasting (used in particular in Europe)
412	**DUB**
413	**DAM**
413	**D**owned **A**ir**C**raft
413	**DUC** [(Latin) lead - e.g. aqueduct]
414	**DAD**
414	**D**rinking **A**nd **D**riving
414	**DUD** (fireworks display)
414	*Dungeons And Dragons*
415	**DAY**
415	**DUE**
415	to**DAY**
416	**D**eep **A**ir **S**trike
416	**D**epartment of the **A**ir **F**orce
416	**D**eparture **A**ir**F**ield
416	**D**octor-**A**ssisted **S**uicide
417	**DAG** (hanging shred)
417	**DUG** (teat, udder; completed excavation)
418	**DAH** (dash in morse code)
418	**DUH**
418	o**DAH** [(Turkish) a room in a harem]
419	**DAN** (skill level in martial arts)
419	**DUI** [(410 DUO-pl) instrumental duets]
419	**DUN** (a dull brown colour; to demand payment)
420	**D**ead **L**etter **O**ffice (retains undeliverable mail)
421	**D**ual **L**aser **U**nit (displayed over or through Location)
422	**D**ead-**L**etter **B**ox (dead drop, often in unused Location)
422	**D**inner, **B**ed and **B**reakfast
422	**D**ou**BL**e
422	**D**ouble **B**ed and **B**reakfast
424	**DVD**
425	deci**BE**ls (rock concert)
426	**D**estroyed **B**y **F**ire
426	**D**isney**L**and **P**ark

446	Dust Detection System (such systems in dusty areas)
448	Diamond Drill Hole (exploration stage of mining)
448	Dual Doppler Radar
449	Don't Do It (evil, stupid crime)
450	Data-Entry Terminal (Objects visible on screen)
450	DETached (8 House)
451	oDEA (pl.of ODEUM: buildings for the performance of vocal and instrumental music)
452	DEV (Hindu god; -elopment)
452	oDYL (=OD, the vital force)
453	DECimal
453	DEW
454	Data Entry Display
454	DEX (sulphate used as a stimulant)
455	DEY (former North African ruler)
455	DYE
456	DEF (excellent)
456	DEPot
456	DEScent
456	DEStination
456	DEStroyer
456	DYS- (bad)
456	oXES [(pl.) OX, in sense of clumsy person]
457	DEGeneration
457	DEGree(-s)
458	oXER
459	DEN
459	DENmark (Copenhagen)
459	oXEN
460	Deep Sky Object (possible 160 UFO)
460	DeParTment
460	oDSO [(obs.) an interjection expressing surprise - perhaps to announce an ambush]
461	Designated Smoking Area

462	Deep Sand Bed
462	Dry Span Bridge (often laid for military manoeuvres)
463	Department of Public Works
463	Drug-Free Workplace
463	Dry Cask Storage (high-level radioactive waste)
465	Drum Storage Yard
466	Deep Space Probe
466	Deep Space Station
466	Department of Public Prosecutions
466	Department of Social Security
466	Detailed Site Plan
466	Digital Satellite System
466	Discount Furniture Store
466	Drain and Storage System
466	Drug-Free Zone
466	Dry Fuel Storage
466	Duplex Stainless Steel (used in bars, coils, cutlery, hardware, industrial equipment, large building construction material, major appliances, plates, sheets, storage tanks, surgical instruments, tankers, tubing, wires)
466	eXperimental Space Station
468	Deep Sea Research
468	Department of Public Health
469	*Deep Space Nine*
469	DJIbouti (Djibouti)
470	Designated Ground Target
470	Don't Go There
473	Deputy General Manager (0 Office)
474	DGX dogfishes
476	Dangerous Goods Shipping
476	Desired Ground Zero: nuclear detonation target
477	Department of Juvenile Justice
477	*DiG duG*
479	DesiGN
479	DJIbouti (same)
479	Dow-Jones Index

480	Disaster Relief Office
480	Distance = Rate x Time
480	Dive Rescue Team
481	Departure Holding Area
482	Disused Railway Line
483	Dinner Roll Call
484	**DRX** Discontinuous Reception (Location seen like this)
485	**DRY**
486	Data Relay Satellite/Station
486	Destination Rail Station
486	**DR**ive**S** (repeated throughout Location)
487	Degrees, Radians, Grads (key on scientific calculators)
488	Department of Human Resources
488	Digital RailRoad
489	Desert Research Institute, 92 NV
489	Double Helix Nebula
490	**DIT** (dot in Morse code)
490	Do Not Open/Operate
491	Department of Internal Affairs
491	**DIA** [(G) through, between]
491	**DIA**meter
492	**DIB** (to fish)
492	Digital Image Library
492	**DIL**ute
492	**DIV**
493	**DIC** (say, speak)
493	**DIM**
493	o**DIC** (of or pertaining to an ode; hypothetical vital energy)
493	to**XIC**
494	Damsels In Distress
494	**DID**
494	***DnD*** (*Dungeons and Dragons*)

| 495 | **DIE** |
| 495 | **DIY** |

496	**DIF**ference
496	**D**igital **I**maging **S**urveillance/**S**ystem
496	**DIP**
496	**DIS**integration
496	**DIS**placement
496	**DIS**posal
496	**DIS**tance

| 497 | **DIG** |

498	**DIR**ection
498	**DIR**ector (chair/office)
498	**DIR**ectorate
498	**DIR**ectory

499	**DIN**
499	o**DIN** (major god in Norse mythology)
499	to**XIN**

500	End Of Terrace
500	End Of Time
500	End Of Track
500	Indy

501	Electrical Operating Area
501	Levi (Location from commercial)
501	**YOU**

| 502 | End Of Line (subway) |
| 502 | **YOB** |

503	Emergency Operations Center
503	Expeditionary Operations Center
503	ETC.
50C	(flipped half-dollar landing on Location floor)

| 504 | End Of Day |
| 504 | **YOD** (Hebrew letter) |

505	End Of Empire (e.g. Roman)
505	-**ETY** [(L) state or quality of]
505	t**ETE** [(French) an elaborately dressed head of hair; a headdress; a head]

| 506 | Earth Observation Satellite |

506	Earth Observing System
506	Enemy Of the State (on the run)
506	Extra-TerrestrialS

507	Electro-OculoGram: used for retinal dysfunction detection
507	Enhanced Target Graphic (Location through target graphic in greater close-up)
507	Expeditionary Training Group (arriving at and scouting Location in, say, helicopters or a jeeps)

508	Earth Orbit Rendezvous
508	End Of Ramp (Evel Knievel leaping Objects)
508	End Of Road
508	End Of Runway
508	ETHernet (family of frame-based computer networking technologies for 219 Local Area Networks)
508	ETHiopia (Addis Ababa)

509	EON (an indefinitely long period of time; an age)
509	Extra-Terrestrial Intelligence (one of best proofs of its existence is their reluctance to stay on Earth)
509	Young Offender Institution (728 GBR)

510	EAT (diner or restaurant)
510	Emergency Action Team
510	Emergency Area Office
510	tEAT

| 511 | Evacuee Assembly Area (trains from a ghetto or impending war zone) |
| 511 | EAU (French for *water*) |

| 512 | Expeditionary Air Base |
| 512 | tEAL (a kind of duck) |

513	Emergency Action Centre
513	tEAK [(Malayalam) a large tree of the verbona family of India and SE Asia; the timber of this tree, a dark oily wood of great strength and durability]
513	tEAM
513	YAM (plant having an edible root)
513	YAK
513	YAW (angle about the vertical axis; to deviate from the intended course)
513	YUK (to laugh loudly)
513	YUM

| 514 | Elite Athletes with a Disability |

514 EUro Disney, 681 FRAnce

515 Express Auto (used cars) Exchange
515 YAE (Japanese for "doubled" or "multi-layered", often in reference in flowers; a Cyrillic letter)
515 YAY (to this extent)

516 Electronic Article Surveillance (usually at store entries)
516 Emergency Alert (weather) System
516 Etch A Sketch
516 Extensive Air Shower [(many kilometres wide) cascade of ionized particles and electromagnetic radiation produced in the atmosphere when a *primary* cosmic ray (i.e. one of extra-terrestrial origin) enters the atmosphere. The term *cascade* means that the incident particle, a proton, nucleus, an electron, photon, or (rarely) a positron, strikes a molecule in the air and produces many high energy ions (*secondaries*), which in turn create more, and so on; onset of *The Day Of The Triffids*]
516 YAP (to bark shrilly)
516 YUP

517 East Asian Games
517 YAG (Yttrium Aluminium Garnet: synthetic garment)

518 EAR
518 Emergency Action Room
518 EURope
518 tEAR
518 YAH
518 YUH

519 Engine Air Intake (Objects sucked in)

520 Electronic Booking Tool [(probably vacation) Location booked]
520 English Language Teaching
520 Extra-Vehicular Operations (NASA)

521 Electronic Vault Access
521 Extra-Vehicular Activity (space walk)
521 tELA [(Lat.) a web-like structure]

522 EBB (tide going out)
522 Electronic Bulletin Board (arrivals, departures and travel news etc. at an 1 Airport, large 86 Railway Station etc.)
522 English Language Learners (class)
522 tELL (statue of William or him shooting apple off his son's

	head with his crossbow)
522	**Y2K** (Year 2 Thousand)
523	**ELK** (large deer)
523	**ELM** (**EL**ectronic **M**ail; deciduous tree)
523	**E**xecutive **B**oard **M**eeting
524	**E**dge **L**ighted **D**isplay
524	**E**gyptian **B**ook of the **D**ead
524	**ELD** (old age)
524	**EL**ectro-luminescent **D**isplay
524	**E**nd **O**f **B**usiness **D**ay (88 Rush Hour)
525	**EVE**
525	**EVE**ning
525	t**ELE** [(abbr.) TV; (G) far, at or to a distance]
526	**E**lectronic **B**attle**F**ield
526	**ELF**
526	**E**mergency **L**anding **P**latform
526	**E**mergency **L**anding **S**ite
526	**E**xtreme **L**ong **S**hot (cinematography)
526	**E**xtremely **L**ow **F**requency (radiation frequencies from 3 to 30 Hz)
528	**E**arly **L**ife **H**istory
528	**E**xtra-**V**ehicular **R**obotics
529	**E**lectron **B**eam **I**maging/**I**rradiation
529	**E**lectronic **B**rain **I**maging
530	**ECO**logy
530	**E**lectro-**C**onvulsive **T**herapy
530	**E**ngineering, **C**onstruction & **O**perations
531	**E**arth-**C**rossing **A**steroids
531	**ECU** (old French coin)
531	**ECU**ador (Quito)
531	**EMU** (large, flightless bird)
531	**E**xtreme **C**lose **U**p
532	**EMB**assy
533	**E**arly **C**hildhood **C**enter
534	**E**lectronic **M**ap **D**isplay
535	**EKE**

535	**EME** (uncle)
535	**E**mpty **C**ontainer **Y**ard (3 Warehousing)
535	**EWE**
535	t**EME** [(obs.) team]
535	t**YKE** (a dog, a cur; a rough-mannered person, esp. a Roman Catholic)
536	**E**ntry **C**ontrol **P**oint
536	t**EMP**
536	t**EMS** (a sieve)
536	t**YMP** (the plate of a blast furnace opening)
536	**Y**outh **C**orrectional **F**acility
537	**E**lectro-**C**ardio**G**ram; -**G**raph
538	**E**lectronic **C**ombat **R**ange
538	**E**levator **M**achine **R**oom
538	t**ECH** (poly-; -nology)
540	**E**mergency **D**uty **T**eam
540	**EXT**ension (building)
540	t**EXT**
542	**E**ntry, **D**escent and **L**anding (space vehicles)
543	**E**nduro **X** **C**ountry
543	**E**lectronic **D**esign **C**enter
544	**E**xplosive **D**etection **D**og (sniffing each Object in turn)
545	**EXE**cution
546	**E**arth **D**eparture **S**tage (space vehicles)
546	**E**quipment **D**econtamination **S**ystem
546	**E**xecutive **D**ining **F**acility
546	**EXP**ressway
547	**EX**chan**G**e
548	**E**mployee **D**ining **R**oom
548	**E**xtended **D**uty **H**ours (workplaces - yours or an acquaintances, 6 Factory, 8 Hospital etc.)
550	**E**nergy **E**fficient **T**ransport
550	**E**xtremely **E**lliptical **O**rbit
550	**YET**
551	**YEA** (affirmative vote)

552   **EEL**
552   t**EEL** (the sesame plant)

553   **EEK**
553   t**EEM**
553   **YEM**en (Sana'a)
553   **YEW** (evergreen tree or shrub)

554   **Electron-Explosive Device** (explosive or pyrotechnic component that by the application of electrical energy initiates an explosive, burning, electrical, or mechanical train)

554   **Extreme Emotional Distress/Disturbance**

555   **EYE** (closed-circuit television)
555   t**YEE** (a food fish)

556   **Electrical Equipment Section**
556   o**YES** or o**YEZ** (the call of a public crier for attention before making a proclamation)
556   **YEP**
556   **YES**

557   **Electro-EncephaloGram/-Graphy)**

558   **Elevated Equipment Room**
558   **Escape, Evacuation and Rescue**
558   o**YER** (a hearing or an inspection, as of a deed, bond, etc. as when a defendant in court prays oyer of a writing)
558   t**EER** (to daub, plaster)
558   t**YER** (one who ties)
558   **YEH** (Yeah)

559   **YEN** (to yearn)
559   t**EEN** (injury, pain; to injure; a 8 Hospital or sports clinic)

560   **EFT** (newt)
560   **Electro-Shock Therapy**
560   **Elevated Storage Tank**
560   **EST**ate(s)
560   **EST**onia (Tallinn)
560   t**EST** (Time-Evac-Signal-Time: potential evacuation of a commercial flight)
560   t**YPO** (a typographical error)

561   **Emergency Services Unit**

561	ESA El SAlvador (San Salvador)
561	Extended Service Area
561	tESA (an organophosphorus compound used as an insect sterilant and formerly to treat cancer)

| 562 | Empire State Building |

| 564 | Emergency Shut-Down (Location suddenly in emergency lighting with alternative air supply) |

| 565 | tYPE (Location in printed letters) |
| 565 | tYPY (characterised by conformity to a group) |

566	Employee Self Service
566	ESP
566	ESP Spain (Madrid)
566	-ESS
566	tESS [(Amharic) an Ethiopian cereal grass]
566	tYPP (a unit of yarn size)

| 568 | Elderly People's Home |

| 569 | EPI- [(G) upon, at, in addition] |

| 570 | Eccentric orbiting Geophysical Observatory |
| 570 | EGO (conscious self; I) |

| 571 | tEGU [(Aztec) a large black and yellow South American lizard] |

| 573 | Executive Golf Course |
| 573 | Extraordinary General Meeting |

| 575 | EGYpt (Cairo) |

| 577 | EGG |
| 577 | tEGG (a sheep in its second year) |

| 578 | Emergency Generator Room |
| 578 | EnGineeRing |

| 579 | You Got It |

| 580 | tYRO [(Lat.) a novice or beginner] |

581	ERA
581	Explosive Reactive Armour
581	Emergency Housing Unit

581	Emergency Relief/Response Unit
582	Electronic Resources Library
582	Enhanced Radiation (neutron) Bomb
583	Equipment Repair Centre
583	tERM
585	ERE (previous to; before)/'ERE
585	tYRE
585	TYRE (292 LIB Lebanon)
586	Earthquake Hazard Zone
586	Electronic Repair Plant
586	Emergency Relocation Site
586	ERS [European climbing plant (ervil)]
587	ERG (wind-swept area of broad, flat desert with little or no vegetative cover; unit of work or energy)
588	Education and Health Records
588	ERR
588	tEHR (a Himalayan wild goat)
589	ERItrea (Asmara)
589	ERN (one of several European sea-eagles)
589	tERN (a long-winged aquatic bird, related to the gulls)
590	ENT
590	ENTertainment
590	ENTrance
590	tENT (circus, large local gathering)
591	Earth Incidence Angle (at which the Sun's rays strike)
592	tEIL [(Biblical) an oak-like hardwood tree, the *terebinth*, which when cut exudes a fragrant resinous juice]
593	Eat-In Kitchen (when describing an apartment)
593	Effects of Nuclear Weapons
593	ENClosure (e.g. cattle ranch)
594	END
594	tEND (to be disposed or inclined)
595	ENEmy (stalking location)
595	tENE [(arch.) injury, pain]

596	**YIP** (to help)
597	**ENG**ineering
598	**EN**-route **H**olding area
599	t**YIN** (a monetary unit of Kyrgyzstan)
599	**YIN** [feminine passive participle (Chinese)]
600	**POO**
600	**POT** [(Latin) be able]
600	**ZOO**
601	**S**ole-**O**ccupancy **U**nit (single apartment)
601	**STA**tion
602	**F**aster **T**han **L**ight
602	**FOB** (to deceive)
602	**F**ortress **O**f **S**olitude (*Superman*)
602	**F**reight **O**n **B**oard
602	**POL**and (Warsaw)
602	**SOB**
602	**SOL** [(Latin) alone, Sun; fifth tone of diatonic music]
602	**SOL**omon Islands (Honiara)
603	**F**light **T**raining **C**entre
603	**POW**
603	**S**chool **O**f **M**edicine
603	**S**ewage **T**reatment **W**orks
603	**S**ewers **O**f **M**ars
603	**SOM**alia (Mogadishu)
603	**SOW**
603	**ST**oc**K**
604	**FOX** (to outwit)
604	**POD**
604	**POX** (to infect with syphilis)
604	**SOD**
604	**SOX**
605	**FOE**
605	**FOY** (farewell feast or gift)
605	**SOY**(-bean)
605	**STY**
606	**FOP** (to deceive)
606	**P**laster **O**f **P**aris
606	**P**oint **O**f **P**urchase

606	**POP**
606	**POS** [(Latin) place]
606	**STP S**ao **T**ome and **P**rincipe (Sao Tome)
606	**SOP** (to dip or soak in a liquid)
606	**SOS**
607	**FOG**
607	**SOG**
608	**FOR** [(E) before]
608	**POR**tugal (Lisbon)
608	**S**evere **O**ff-**R**oad (e.g. rally)
608	**S**ydney **O**pera **H**ouse, 116 **AUS**tralia
609	**FON** (warm, dry wind)
609	**POI** (Hawaiian food)
609	**SON** [(Latin) sound]
610	**F**orest **A**nd **T**rees
610	**PAT** (father)
610	**PUT** (-ting green)
610	**PUT** (-ty)
610	**SAT**
611	**S**atellite **A**ccumulation **A**rea (orbital junkyard of discarded satellites)
612	**FAB** (something fabricated)
612	**F**lesh **A**nd **B**lood
612	**-FUL** [(E) full of]
612	o**PAL** (an amorphous variety of silica)
612	**PAL**
612	**PUB**
612	**SAL** (salt)
612	**SUB** [to act as a substitute; (L) under; -urb, -marine]
613	**FAC** (make, do)
613	**PAC** (shoe patterned after a moccasin)
613	**PAK**istan (Islamabad)
613	**PAW** (giant or trail of such prints)
613	**SAC** (pouch-like structure in an animal or plant)
613	**SAM**oa (Apia)
613	**SAW**
613	**SUK** [marketplace (souk)]
613	**SUM**
613	**ZAM**bia (Lusaka)
614	**FAD** (passing fancy)

614	**FAX**
614	**FUD**
614	**PAD** (apartment, launch, landing)
614	**PAX** (ceremonial embrace given to signify Christian love and unity)
614	**PUD**
614	**SAD**
614	**SAX** (sound of busker's such echoing throughout the Location)
614	**SUD**an (Khartoum)
614	**ZAX** (tool for cutting roof slates)
615	**FAY** (to join closely)
615	**PAY**
615	**SAE**
615	**SAY**
615	**SUE** (to institute legal proceedings against)
616	o**PUS** [(Lat.) work, esp. an artistic or literary work]
616	**PAP** (soft food for infants)
616	**PUP** (to give birth to puppies)
616	**PUS** (viscous fluid formed in infected tissue)
616	**SAP**
616	**SUP**
616	to**PAZ**
616	**ZAP**
616	**ZAS** (pizzas)
617	**FAG**
617	**FAQ**
617	**FUG** (a vast, aging, multi-storied tenement building)
617	**PUG** (to fill in with clay or mortar)
617	**SAG**
617	**SUQ** [marketplace (souk)]
617	**ZAG** (to turn sharply)
618	**FAR**
618	**FUR**
618	o**PAH** (a large sea-fish with laterally flattened body)
618	**PAH**!
618	**PAR**
618	**PAR**aguay (Asuncion)
618	**PUR PU**erto **R**ico (619 San Juan)
618	Sea/**A**ir **R**escue
618	**SUR**iname (Paramaribo)
618	t**SAR** [(Russian) ruler, emperor; Bomb, 1961]
619	**FAN**

619	**FUN** (party)
619	**PAN**ama (City)
619	**PUN**
619	**SUI** Switzerland (Bern)
619	**SUN**
620	**PLO**
620	Sea Based Terminal
620	**SLO**venia (Ljubljana)
621	Fighter Bomber Attack
621	**FLU**
621	Small Business Unit
623	**PLW** Palau (Melekeok)
623	**PVC**
623	Short Loan Collection
623	**SVK** SloVaKia (Bratislava)
624	Fie**LD**
624	SnowBoard **X** (cross)
625	**FLY** (clever; to hit a ball high into the air in baseball)
625	**PLE** PaLEstine
625	**PLY**
625	**SLE** Sierra LEone (Freetown)
625	**SLY**
625	Strength-Building Exercises
625	Synthetic Battlespace Environment (modelling and simulation)
626	Special Boat Service
626	Student Book Store
627	*Fat Bottomed Girls* (in a 26 Bicycle Race)
627	**SL**ud**G**e
627	Supersonic Business Jet
628	Sea Level Height/Rise
628	Self Loading Rifle (sight roving Objects)
628	Small Boat Harbor
628	Small Luxury Hotel
628	Supermassive Black Hole
629	**FBI**
629	Small and Large Intestine
629	Space-Based Interceptor

630	For Members Only (exclusive club)
630	SuMmiT
630	Supreme CourT
631	SCArsdale (historic abode of the rich and famous, 95 New York)
631	Shuttle Carrier Aircraft
631	SKA (Jamaican music)
631	Snow-Covered Area
631	Stairs of Cirith Ungol, Middle-Earth
632	Printed Circuit Board: the central one is motherboard in many modern computers (Location *a la Tron* in form of one)
632	Process Control Board (usually for purposes of work co-ordinations, including such things as information grids and flow charts)
635	SKY
635	SWEden (Stockholm)
636	SWZ SWaZiland (Lobamba/Mbabane)
637	Slow Crack Growth
638	SMR San MaRino (City of San Marino)
639	SCaN
639	SKN Saint Kitts and Nevis (Basseterre)
639	Special Care Nursery
643	Swingers' Date Club
645	FEdEx
645	FounDrY
646	Portable Document Format: often-convertible files made with program Acrobat)
646	Same Day Surgery
646	Slurry Delivery System (pouring onto Location)
648	Student Dining Room
649	Strategic Defence Initiative
650	FET (to fetch)
650	PET
650	SET

651	**FEU** (to grant land to under Scottish feudal law)
651	**PEA**
651	**SEA**
652	**SEL** [(-f); (French: salt)]
652	**SYL** (with, together)
653	**FEM** (passive homosexual)
653	**FEW**
653	**PEC** (-toral muscle)
653	**PEW**
653	**SEC** (-ant)
653	**SEC**urity
653	**SEW**
653	**ZEK** (inmate in a Soviet labour camp)
654	**FED**eral agent
654	**PED** (natural soil aggregate; foot)
654	**PYX** [container for the Eucharist; (also: 694 PIX)]
654	**SEX**
655	**FEE**
655	**FEY** (giving an impression of vague unworldliness; having supernatural powers of clairvoyance; fated to die or at the point of death)
655	**PEE**
655	**PYE** (book of ecclesiastical rules in the pre-Reformation English church)
655	**SEE**
655	**SEY**chelles (Victoria)
656	**FEZ** (brimless cap worn by men in the Near East)
656	**PEP**
656	**S**urface **E**ffect **S**hip (had both an air cushion, like a hovercraft, and twin hulls, like a catamaran)
656	**ZEP** (long sandwich)
657	**PEG**
657	**SEG** (advocate of racial segregation)
657	**SEG**ment
658	**FEH**! (expression of distaste)
658	**PER** [for each; (L) through]
658	**PER**u (Lima)
658	**SER**mon
658	**SER**vice
658	**SYR**ia (Damascus)
658	to**PER** (drinker)

659	**FEN**
659	**FYI**
659	o**PEN**
659	**PEN** (Protons+ Electrons- Neutrons: neutral parts of an atom; monetary unit of Japan)
659	**SEI** [whale (rorqual)]
659	**SEN**egal (Dakar)
659	**SYN** [-e; (G) together]
660	Flatter Squarer Tube
660	o**PPO** [a partner; an (military rather than surgical) operation]
660	**PST**!
660	Social Security Office
661	o**SSA** [(pl.) bone]
661	**SPA**
662	San Fernando Valley, 21 LA
662	Social Sciences Building
662	Space Ship Line
662	Steam Ship Line
663	**FSM** Micronesia
663	Super Star Cluster
664	Fuel Supply Depot
664	**SFX**
664	Super Star Destroyer (*The Empire Strikes Back*)
665	Shanghai Stock Exchange, 389 CHN
665	Solar System Exploration
665	**SPY**
666	number of the Beast
666	**PSP**
666	Sea Scout Ship
666	Self-Storage Facility
666	Side Scan Sonar
666	**ZZZ** (snoring)
667	Putt Putt Golf
667	Special Patrol Group
668	Secure Storage Room
669	**PSI** (-onics)

671	PGA (golf)
673	Finished Goods Warehouse
673	Persian Gulf War
673	Precision Guided Weapons
674	Secure Gold Deposit
675	Parachute Jumping Exercise
675	Small Group Exercise
676	Primary Ground Station
676	Satellite Ground Station
677	ShaGGy
678	SunGlass Hut
679	SiGN
680	FoRT
680	FRO (away)
680	PHT! (intj.used to an expression of mild anger or annoyance)
680	PRO [(L) in front of, favouring]
680	SHeeT
680	SHOwtime
681	Field Replaceable Unit
681	FRAnce (Paris)
681	Passenger Hold Area
682	Federal Reserve Bank
682	Second Hand Books
682	SRB SeRBia (Belgrade)
682	Sydney Harbour Bridge, 116 AUStralia
683	PRK North Korea (Pyongyang) (308 KOR South KORea)
683	Public Health Centre
684	FoRD
684	PhD
684	SHelter Deck (naval architecture)
685	FRY
685	PRE- [(L) before]
685	PRY
685	SHE
685	SHY

685	Spontaneous Human Explosion
686	Fantasy Role Playing
686	Field Research Facility
686	Fire and Rescue Service
686	Second Hand Smoke (tainting the Location)
686	Ship Repair Facility
686	State Historic Park
687	FoRGe
687	Self Help Group
688	PRaiRie
688	School Repair and Renovation
688	Search and Rescue Region
688	SHH
688	SHoRe
688	Short Range Radio
689	PHIlippines (Manila)
689	SRI Lanka (Sri Jayawardenapura-Kotte)
690	FIT (a gym)
690	PIT (a mine; to mark with cavities or depressions)
690	SIT
690	ZIT
691	Files and Information Unit
691	PIA (brain membrane)
692	FIB
692	Food N' Beverage
692	SIB(-ling)
692	SNowBoarding
692	Surface Nuclear Burst
693	FIC (make, do)
693	PIC
693	Public Information Centre
693	SIC (said in context; to urge to attack)
693	SIM(-ulation; -ulator)
694	FID (topmast support bar)
694	FIX
694	FrieNDly (sports match)
694	PIX [container for the Eucharist (also: 654 PYX); an exhibition or museum]
694	SouND (a narrow stretch of water forming an inlet or

connecting two wider areas of water such as two seas or a sea and a lake)

695	**FIE** (interjection expressing disapproval, e.g. *Jack And The Beanstalk* giant)
695	**PIE** (Power = Current x Voltage)
695	**S**evere **N**oise **E**nvironment (manufacturing and repair plant; a rock concert)
695	**S**uper**N**ova**E**
696	**-oSIS** (process or condition of)
696	**PIP** (to break through the shell of an egg)
696	**S**ilent **I**ndividual **S**tudy
696	**SIP** (a bar)
696	**SIS**
696	**SN**i**P**er/**S**niper **N**ight **S**ight (roving Objects)
696	**ZIP**
697	**FIG** (to adorn)
697	**FIJ**i (Suva)
697	**PIG**
697	**PNG** Papua New Guinea (Port Moresby)
697	**S**pecial **I**nterest **G**roup
697	**ZIG**
698	**FIR** (evergreen tree)
698	**SIR** (private school)
699	**FIN**
699	**FIN**ance
699	**FIN**al (sports match)
699	**FIN**land (Helsinki)
699	**PIN**
699	**SIN**
699	**SIN**gapore (Singapore)
699	**ZIN**fadel
700	**GOO**
700	**GOT**
700	**GOT**ham (*Batman*)
700	**JOT**
701	**GOA** (Asian gazelle)
701	**G**ulf **O**f 13 AK **AL**aska
701	**J**oan **O**f **A**rc (battle)
702	**GOB** (to fill a pit with waste)
702	**G**roup **O**f **B**locks (apartments)

702	**JOB**

703	Gulf Of 354 MEXico
703	**JOW** (to toll)

704	**GOD**
704	Good Old Days
704	**GOX** (gaseous oxygen)

705	**GOY** (non-Jewish person)
705	**JOY**

706	Ground Tracking Station

707	**JOG**

708	**GOR** (setting for series of fantasy novels by John Norman; interjection used as a mild oath)
708	**JOR**dan (Amman)

710	**GAT** (pistol - shooting chunks off each Object)
710	Ground Assault Tank (*The Phantom Menace*)
710	**GUT** (a boxing match)
710	**JUT**
710	**QAT** (evergreen shrub; also: 310 KAT)
710	**QAT**ar (Doha)
710	**QUO**

711	**GUA**temala (Guatemala City)
711	**QUA** (in the capacity of)

712	**GAB**
712	**GAB**on (Libreville)
712	**GAL**
712	**GUL** (design in oriental carpets)
712	**GUV**
712	**JAB**
712	Joint Assault Bridge
712	Jules Undersea Lodge, 62 FL

713	**GAM** (to visit socially)
713	**GAM**bia (Banjul)
713	**GUM**
713	**GUM GU**aM (Hagatna)
713	**JAM** (group improvisation, traffic)
713	**JAM**aica (Kingston)
713	**JAW**

714 **GAD** (to roam about restlessly)

715 **GAE** (to go)
715 **GAY**
715 **G**eneral **U**rine **E**xamination
715 **GUY**
715 **GUY**ana (Georgetown)
715 **JAY**

716 **GAP**
716 **GAS**
716 **GUP** [(India and the Far East) gossip, tattle, scandal]
716 **JUS** (legal right)

717 **GAG**
717 **JAG** (to cut unevenly; cleaning tool for firearms)
717 **JUG**

718 **GAR** (to compel)
718 **G**round **U**nder **R**epair
718 **JAR**

719 **GUN**
719 **GUI**nea (Conakry)

720 **G**round **B**ased **O**bservatory
720' (double spin)

721 **G**eneral **B**usiness **U**nit
721 *The **G**ood, The **B**ad & The **U**gly*

722 **G**lass **B**ottom **B**oat
722 **G**round-**B**ased **L**aser

723 **G**roup **L**earning **C**entre

724 **GL**i**D**er (circling then landing upon Location, *a la Escape From New York*)
724 **G**o**LD**

725 **G**ro**VE**
725 o**GLE**

726 **GBS** **G**uinea-**B**i**S**sau (Bissau)
726 **G**eneral **B**uilding **P**lan
726 **G**o**LF**

727 **G**eo**L**o**G**y

728	GBH
728	GLaRe
728	Great Barrier Reef
728	GReat Britain (London)
729	GLeN (narrow valley)
729	Global Bridge Net (Internet in 389 CHiNa)
729	Greyhound Lines, Inc.
730	General Military Training
730	Grand Central Terminal, 953 NYC
730	Ground Cavalry Troops
730	JunCTion
732	George Washington Bridge, 95 NY and 97 NJ
732	JCB
735	GateWaY
736	Grand Central Station, 953 NYC
736	Ground Control Station
736	Guided Missile Station
737	Boeing
738	Gas-Cooled Reactor
738	Grand Canyon Railway, 16 AZ
742	Guide Dogs for the Blind
743	Juvenile Detention Center
745	GuiDE
745	GalaXY
746	Gasoline Dispensing Facility (gas station)
746	GuarDS
747	Boeing
748	Giant Death Robot
749	GarDeN
750	GEO [(Latin) earth]
750	GEOrgia (Tbilisi)
750	GET

750	**JET**
751	**JEU** [(French) game - a sports match or pastime taking place in 781 FRAnce]
752	**GEL**
752	**G**od's **E**ye View (aviation)
752	**QE2**
753	**GEM**
753	**GYM**
753	**JEW**
754	**GED** (food fish)
754	**G**lobal **EX**change
755	**GEE/JEE** (to turn right - a right-hand turn)
755	o**GEE** (a curve or moulding-like integral sign; arch of two curves meeting at a point)
756	**GYP** (swindle; also 796 GIP)
757	**GEQ** Equatorial Guinea (Malabo)
758	**G**enetically **E**ngineered/**E**nhanced **H**uman
758	**GER**many (Berlin)
759	**GEN** (knowledge attained by investigation)
759	**GEN**esis
760	**G**eneral **P**ost **O**ffice
760	**G**eostationary **S**atellite **O**rbit
762	**G**eneral **P**urpose **B**oat
762	**G**reat **S**alt **L**ake
763	**G**un **S**hot **W**ound(s)
765	**G**round **S**upport **E**quipment (aircraft)
766	**G**as **F**ired **S**tation
766	**G**eneral **P**urpose **F**acility
766	**G**eo-**S**tationary **S**atellite
766	**G**un**F**ire **S**upport
767	**JPG** (graphics file type/extension)
769	**G**roup **F**itness **I**nstructor

769	**JPN JaPaN** (Tokyo)
772	**G**olden **G**ate **B**ridge, 66 SF
775	**G**reat **G**lass **E**levator
776	**G**as **G**athering **S**tation
777	**G**imme! x3
777	**G**o! x3
777	**G**oing, **G**oing, **G**one
780	**G**roup **R**apid **T**ransit
781	**GHA**na (Accra)
781	**G**rid **R**eference **U**nit
782	**GR**o**V**e
784	**G**ua**RD**
785	**GRE**ece (Athens)
785	o**GRE** (a cannibalistic giant)
787	General **HQ** (military)
788	**G**iant **R**esource **R**ecovery (recycling plant)
789	**GHI** [liquid butter made in India (ghee)]
789	**GRN GR**e**N**ada (St. George's)
789	Jou**RN**alism (9 Newsfloor)
790	**GIT**
791	**GNU** (large antelope)
791	**J**apanese **I**mperial **A**rmy
792	**GIB** (to fasten with a wedge)
792	**JIB** (to refuse to proceed further)
794	**GID** (disease of sheep)
795	**GIE** (to give)
796	**GIP** (swindle; also: 756 GYP)
797	**GIG** (a rock concert; to catch fish with a prolonged spear)
797	**JIG**

798   Global Nuclear Response

799   **GIN**
799   (to be-) **GIN**
799   **JIN** [Muslim supernatural being (jinn)]

800   **HOO** (Sutton, England: Anglo-Saxon burial site)
800   **HOT**
800   **ROT** (aging, musty, rain-sodden vast building)
800   t**ROT**

801   Horn Of Africa (peninsula containing the North East African countries of 589 ERItrea, 479 DJIbouti, 508 ETHiopia and 603 SOMalia)
801   Range and Training Area
801   Read Only Area
801   Remotely Operated Aircraft
801   **ROU** Romania (Bucharest)
801   t**HOU**

802   Right-To-Left (Objects - perhaps simultaneously - flopped or rotated on their horizontal perceptual axis)
802   **HOB**
802   **ROB**

803   Hall Of Mirrors
803   **HOW**
803   **ROC** (legendary bird of prey)
803   **ROM** (**R**ead **O**nly **M**emory; male gypsy)
803   **ROW** (48 Death ~; of houses; dispute)
803   t**ROW** (to believe)

804   **HOD**
804   **ROD**
804   t**ROD** (track, path)

805   **HOE**
805   **HOY** (heavy barge)
805   **ROE** (mass of eggs within a female fish)
805   t**ROY** [a system of weights (from **TROY**es in France)]
805   **TROY** (18 TURkey)

806   **HOP** (dance or dance party; router or gateway)

807   Hand Of God
807   **HOG**
807   **ROG** (ask, question, seek)

807	t**ROG** (to trudge, walk wearily)
808	**H**alls **O**f **R**esidence
808	**HOH**?
808	**H**ouses **O**f **H**ealing, Middle-Earth
808	**R**un **O**ff **R**iver (hydroelectric power systems)
809	**HON**
809	**HON**duras (Tegucigalpa)
809	t**RON** [(Scottish) a public weighing-machine for weighing produce in the market-place of a city or burgh; the post of this used as a pillory]
810	**HAT**
810	**H**ead **A**bdomen **T**horax: 3 main insect body parts
810	**HUT**
810	**RAT**
810	**RUT**
810	t**HAT**
810	**TRAT** [(abbreviation) **TRAT**toria, an Italian restaurant]
811	**H**igh **A**ctivity **A**ircraft
811	**H**igh **A**ltitude **A**irship
812	**HAL** (**H**euristically programmed **AL**gorithmic computer)
812	**H**igh **A**ltitude **B**urst (hydrogen bomb test)
812	**HUB**
812	o**RAL**
812	**RUB**
813	**HAM**
813	**HAW** (to turn left)
813	**HUM**
813	o**RAC**
813	**RAM** (breaking into a 3 Castle)
813	**RAW**
813	**RUM**
813	t**HAW**
813	t**RAM** (a device for aligning a piece of machinery; to adjust a machine using a tram)
814	**HAD**
814	o**RAD** (towards the mouth)
814	**RAD**
814	**RAD**iation
814	**RAD**io (broadcast or announcements in Location background)
814	**RAX** (to stretch out)

814   t**HUD**
814   t**RAD**

815   **HAY**
815   **HUE**
815   **RAY**
815   **RUE** [(French) road]
815   t**RAY** (the three in cards or dice)
815   t**RUE**

816   **HAP**
816   **H**ead-**U**p **D**isplay (superimposes data over usual viewpoint)
816   **HUP**! (interjection used to mark a marching cadence)
816   **RAP** [(slang) system of conviction and punishment - police station, court, jail]
816   **RAS** (Ethiopian prince)
816   **R**emote **A**ccess **S**ystem (computer such and, say, remote video cameras for covert surveillance)
816   **RUS**sia (Moscow)
816   t**HUS** (frankincense)
816   to**RUS** (a large convex moulding)
816   t**RAP**

817   **HAG**
817   **H**ome **A**ccess **G**ateway (with security intercom etc.)
817   **HUG**
817   **RAG**
817   **RUG**
817   t**HUG**

818   **HAH**!
818   **RAH** (English slang for a public school snob)
818   **R**escue **A**nd **R**ecovery
818   **R**oyal **A**lbert **H**all, London
818   t**HAR** [(Nepali) a Himalayan goat-like antelope, aka *serow*]

819   **HAI**ti (Port-au-Prince)
819   **HUN**
819   **HUN**gary (Budapest)
819   **RAI** (style of popular 127 **ALG**erian music)
819   **RAN**
819   **RUN** (bobsleigh, ski etc.)

821   **R**ed **L**ight **A**rea (Amsterdam, 954 **NED** Netherlands)

822   **H**ead **B**angers' **B**all
822   **H**ell **B**reak **L**oose
822   **H**ome-**B**ased **B**usiness

823	High Bay Warehouse (often very tall racks)
823	HuLK
824	HoLD
824	ReBuilD
824	Red Light District (Amsterdam, 954 NED Netherlands)
825	High-Build Epoxy [(usually shiny) coating]
825	oRBY
825	oRLE (a border within a shield at a short distance from the edge)
827	Royal Botanical Gardens (353 KEW, England)
828	HarBoR
828	RuBbeR
829	High Velocity Impact (crater from meteor fall)
831	Health Care Administration
831	High Contamination Area (abandoned city of Prypiat, 138 UKRaine; post-nuclear attack ruins)
831	oRCA
831	RWAanda (Kigali)
832	HMV
832	Reinforced Concrete Box (common structure for underground passageways like pedestrian subways, sewage tunnels, utility tunnels, storm drain spillways and catch basins)
833	HMM
833	Reinforced Cement Concrete
833	Roller Compacted Concrete
835	HighWaY
835	HiKE
835	HoME
835	RaCE
835	RailWaY
835	RunWaY
836	High Carbon Steel (very strong, used for springs and high-strength wires)
836	High Class Society (party for the urban wealthy)
837	HKG Hong KonG

838	ReaCH (the stretch of water visible between bends in a river or channel)
838	Residential Care Home
838	Road Crash Rescue
839	Human Computer Interaction
839	Human-Machine Interface
839	ReCoNnaissance
840	Heavy Duty Truck
840	Horse Driving Trials
840	Housing Development Office
840	oRDO (an annual religious calendar with instructions for Mass and office for each day)
841	High Density Area
842	Heavy-Duty Vehicle
842	Horse-Drawn Vehicle
842	Hot Dogs and Buns
843	Rail Diesel Car
846	Holographic Data Storage
846	Red Dot Sight (playing over each Object)
847	RiDGe
848	RaDaR
848	RDR! (machine gun sound)
850	HET
850	High Earth Orbit
850	High Eccentric Orbit
850	High Elliptical Orbiter
850	Real Estate Owned
850	RET (to soak in order to loosen the fibre from the woody tissue)
850	RETail
850	RETurn
851	Rocket Engine Assembly
851	RYA (Scandanavian hand-woven rug)
852	REB (Confederate soldier)
852	RELigion
852	REV (-olution)

853	**HEM**
853	**HEW**
853	**REC** (-reation Ground)
853	**REM** (quantity of ionizing radiation)
853	t**HEM**
853	t**HEW** (muscle, strength)
853	t**REK**
854	**HEX** (-agon-shaped building or room; a curse)
854	o**RYX** (a kind of antelope)
854	**RED**
854	**REX** (reigning king; a cat with curly fur that lacks guard hairs)
855	**HEE** (laugh)
855	**HEY**
855	**REE** (female Eurasian sandpiper)
855	**RYE** (cereal rug)
855	t**HEE**
855	t**HEY**
855	t**REE**
855	t**REY** (the three in cards or dice)
856	**HEP**
856	**HES** (male people)
856	**H**ome **E**xercise **P**rogram
856	**H**ydro-**E**lectric **P**ower
856	**REF**
856	**REP** (cross-ribbed ribbon)
856	**RES** (thing or matter)
856	**RES**idence
856	t**REF** [(Hebrew) in the Jewish religion, forbidden as food, not kosher]
856	t**RES** (very)
856	t**REZ** (the three in cards or dice)
858	**HER**
859	**HEN**
859	**H**igh-**E**xplosive **I**ncendiary
859	t**HEN**
860	**H**igh **S**peed **T**rain
860	**H**oi**ST**
860	o**RZO** [(Italian) pasta in the form of small pieces like barley]
860	**R**ailway **S**orting **O**ffice (on a moving train)

861	Regional PArk
861	Road Side Accident
861	**RSA** South Africa (Pretoria/executive; Bloemfontein/judicial; Cape Town/legislative)

862	High-Speed Bus
862	High Speed Vehicle
862	ReSerVe

863	Health and Fitness Club
863	High-Performance Computing
863	High Speed Chase
863	High Speed Craft
863	**RPM**

864   Heat Sensing Device (played over each Object)

865	HouSE
865	Hull Planning Yard
865	oRFE [(German) a kind of carp]

866	Heat Power Plant
866	Hydro Power Plant
866	Rescue and Fire Fighting

| 867 | HouSinG (tenement buildings) |
| 867 | Role-Playing Game |

868	High Speed Rail
868	Home Shopping Network
868	RePaiR

870   Harlem Globe Trotters

872   Red Green Blue: the 3 primary colors that in combination create all of the colors in computer and TV displays

875   oRGY

876   HgS (cinnabar: the common ore of mercury)

877   *Hitchhiker's Guide to the Galaxy*

| 878 | HanGaR |
| 878 | RanGeRs |

| 880 | Hostage Rescue Team |
| 880 | Right Hand Traffic |

880	t**HRO** [(arch.) through]
881	Hard Hat Area
881	o**RRA** [(Scottish) odd, not matched. An *orra man* is a farm-worker kept to do any odd job that may arise]
881	Records Holding Area (archive)
881	t**HRU** [(arch.) through]
884	High Resolution Display (entire image sometimes displayed on bank of many flush screens)
884	RailHeaD (railway line terminus that interfaces with another transport mode such as an airport or a ferry terminal)
885	Homeless and Runaway Youth
885	Residential Real Estate
888	**HRH**
889	Human-Robot Interaction
890	**HIT**
890	Hole In One
890	t**HIO** [(of compounds) containing sulphur]
890	t**RIO**
891	o**HIA** [(Hawaiian) a Polynesian tree of the myrtle family with bright red flowers, aka *lehua*]
891	**RIA** (long, narrow inlet)
892	Rhythm N' Blues
892	**RIB**
892	**RIV**
893	**HIC**
893	Hazardous Industrial Waste
893	High Intensity Conflict
893	**HIM**
893	**RIM**
893	t**RIM**
894	**HID**
894	**RID**
895	**HIE** (to hurry)
896	**HIP**
896	**HIS**
896	**HIS** (-tory)

896	Rest In Peace
896	RIF (to lay off from employment by eliminating the position)
896	RIP
896	tHIS
896	tRIP
897	RIG
897	RaNGe (firing)
897	tRIG (-onometry)
898	Rest N' Relaxation
899	RIN (to run or melt)
899	tHIN (all Objects optically squeezed along the horizontal axis)
899	tRIN (a triplet by birth)
900	NOT
900	oNTO
901	ITAly (Rome)
901	Not Often Used
901	Nuclear Test Aircraft (Objects below as testing zone in airborne burst)
902	Interplanetary Transfer Vehicle
902	Navy Operating Base
902	NOB
903	NOW
904	NOD (nodding donkeys or pumpjacks station)
905	-ITY [(L) state or quality of]
905	Nap Of the Earth (very low-altitude flight course used by military aircraft to avoid enemy detection and attack)
906	In The Flesh
906	In The Future
906	Inside The Perimeter
906	ITS
906	Naval OPerations
906	NV 92 NeVada Test Site
906	tITS
907	NOG (strong ale; to fill space with bricks)

908	**NOH** (classical drama of Japan)
908	**NOR**
908	**NOR**way (Oslo)
908	**NTH** (pertaining to item number *n*)
909	In **O**rbit **I**nfrastructure
909	**ION** (electrically charged atom)
909	**-ION** [(L) condition or action of]
909	**NON** (not)
909	t**ITI** (a small South American monkey)
910	In **A**nd **O**ut
910	**NUT**
911	emergency service
912	**-IAL** [(L) relating to]
912	**I**nternal **A**ffairs **B**ureau
912	**NAB**
912	**NAV**y
912	**NUB**
913	**I**mage **A**nalysis **C**enter
913	**NAM**ibia (Windhoek)
913	**NAW**
913	**NUC**lear
914	**I**nternal **A**ffairs **D**ivision
914	**NAD**
915	**NAY**
916	Inter-**U**rban **S**tructure
916	**I**nternational **A**ir**P**ort
916	**NAP** (of the Earth)
916	o**NUS**
917	**NAG**
918	**NAH**
918	**NUR**sing
918	t**IAR** (a tiara)
919	**-IAN** [(L) practitioners or inhabitants]
919	**NAN** [Indian flat round leavened bread; (L) the nature of]
919	**NUN**
920	In**B**ound **T**ransportation

920   tILT (certain kinds of train)

921   **NBA**
921   No Longer Used

922   **ILL**
922   **ILL**umination
922   **IVB** British Virgin Islands (Road Town)
922   t**ILL**

923   **ILK**
923   Industrial Light and Magic
923   Interactive VideoConferencing
923   Nuclear Biological Chemical: primary types of national defence

925   **-IVE** [(L) nature of]
925   **IVY** (climbing vine)
925   Night Vision Equipment
925   o**NLY**
925   t**ILE**
925   t**IVY** (with great speed, like a 160 UFO escaping Earth defences)

926   Information and Library Service
926   Integrated Bridge System
926   National Book Store

927   Night Vision Goggles (objects seen via)

928   Normal Business Hours

931   Intensive Care Unit
931   **NCA** Ni**CA**ragua (Managua)
931   t**IKA** [(Hindi) a red mark or pendant on the forehead of Hindu women, originally of religious significance but now also worn for ornament]
931   To**NKA**

932   Infantry Carrier Vehicle
932   No Man's Land

933   **ICK**! (expressing distaste)
933   t**ICK** (any of the small bloodsucking mites of the Acarina order)

934   Incompletely Knocked Down
934   Inland Container Depot

935	**ICE/ICY**
935	o**NCE**
935	t**IME**
936	**IMP** (to graft feathers onto a bird's wing)
936	**I**ndependent **K**arate **S**chool
938	**ICH** (fish disease)
938	t**ICH** (a small person)
939	**N**ear **M**iss **I**ncident
939	t**IKI** [(Maori) in Polynesia, an image representing an ancestor, often worn as an amulet; to take a scenic tour round an area]
944	**I**nterim **D**ry-**D**ocking
945	**IDE**
945	**N**ear **D**eath **E**xperience
945	t**IDE**
945	t**IDY**
946	**I**ntermediate **D**istribution **F**rame
950	**N**ear-**E**arth **O**bject
950	**NEO**
950	**NET**
951	**N**aval **E**xercise **A**rea
951	**N**ear-**E**arth **A**steroid
951	**NEU**tral (merchant ship)
952	**NEB** (bird beak)
952	**NYL**on
953	**NYC**, 95 **NY**
953	**NEW**
954	**NED NE**therlan**D**s (Amsterdam)
954	o**NYX**
955	**NEE**
955	**N**ew **Y**ear's **E**ve
956	**N**aval **E**xpeditionary **F**orce
956	**NEP**al (Kathmandu)
956	*Never Ending Story*

957 NEG (photographic evidence)

958 o**NER** (something one of its kind)
958 t**IER**
958 to**NER**

959 **NEI** [(Italian) beauty-spots; birth-marks]

960 Initial Flight Training
960 Inter-Prison Transport
960 **ISO** [(G) equal, same]
960 **-IST** [(G) one who practices]
960 New Store Opening

961 Interim Storage Area
961 No Smoking Area

962 In-Store Bakery
962 **ISL** Iceland (Reykjavik)
962 **ISL**and
962 **ISV** Virgin Islands
962 Naval Submarine Base
962 **NZL** New ZeaLand (Wellington)

963 **-ISM** [(G) quality or doctrine of]

964 Imperial Probe Droid (*The Empire Strikes Back*)

965 **-IFY** [(L) make]
965 Integrated Shipbuilding Environment
965 **-ISE, -IZE** [(G) make, practise, act like]
965 Naval ShipYard

966 **IFF** (if and only if)
966 Independent Power Plant
966 International Space Station
966 **IS**land**S**
966 Nuclear Power Plant/Station
966 Nuclear Storage Facility
966 t**IFF**
966 t**IZZ**

967 Instant Photo Gallery (after theme park ride)

968 In-Flight Refuelling
968 **-ISH** [(E) a similarity or relationship]
968 **ISR**ael (Jerusalam)

969   t**IPI** [(American Indian) a Native American tent]

970   **I**ntegrated **G**lobal **O**cean (Earth largely covered by water)
970   **N**i**G**h**T**

972   **N**atural **G**round **L**evel

973   **I**ndependent **G**arden **C**entre

975   t**IGE** [(French) the shaft of a column]

977   **IGG** (to ignore)

978   **N**ext **G**eneration **H**ighway
978   **NGR** Ni**G**e**R**ia (Abuja)

980   t**IRO** [(Latin) young soldier, new recruit or more generally a novice]

981   **I**ndividual **H**ousing **U**nit
981   **N**ot **R**ecently **U**sed
981   **NRU** Nau**RU** (Yaren)

982   **I**ndustrial **R**o**B**ot (assembly line)
982   **IRL** **IR**e**L**and (Dublin)
982   **N**ational **H**ockey **L**eague

983   **I**ndoor **R**ecreation **C**entre
983   **IRK**

985   **IRE**
985   **N**on-**H**uman **E**ntity
985   **N**on-**R**otating **E**arth
985   t**IRE**

986   **N**ational **H**ealth **S**ervice

987   **IRQ** **IR**a**Q** (Baghdad)

989   **IRI** Iran (Tehran)

990   **NIT** (insect egg)
990   o**INT** (to anoint)
990   t**INT**

991   **INA** **IN**donesi**A** (Jakarta)

992	Never Never Land
992	NIB
992	NIL
993	INK
993	InterNet Cafe
993	NIM (to steal)
993	oINK
993	tINK
994	INDia (New Delhi)
994	INDustry
994	NIX [water sprite; to veto]
994	tIND (to kindle, burn)
995	-INE [(G; L) a compound]
995	tINY
996	INFantry
996	INS (-pection)
996	NIP
996	Not In Service
996	Not In Stock
997	ING
997	NIGer (Niamey)
997	tING
999	INN
999	NIN

GENERATING YOUR OWN LOCATIONS 100-999

This can occur where you need a Location for a page between 100 and 999 but:

*   the page number is not listed in **LOCATIONS 0-999** (because I could not find an acronym that seemed workable)
*   you prefer to only work with Location numbers 0 to 99 from **LOCATIONS 0-999**
*   you wish to use an alternative location to one suggested from **LOCATIONS 0-999** for a page number between 100 and 999

Use the appropriate Location Description from the following table for the first number of the three-digit page number then suffix it with the two-digit Location of your choice:

Number/Associated Letters		Location Description
1	u	uninhabited (empty, but not decaying)
2	b	being built
3	w	windy
4	d	decaying
4	x	forbidden (rated x)
5	e	evening (magic hour)
6	p	polluted
6	s	snow
7	q	queue
8	r	rain/rainbow
9	n	night

Examples:

Page	NLC Code	Location Description	Location 0-99
193	**u**	**u**ninhabited	Internet Cafe

Thus, for page **193** you might picture an **u**ninhabited Internet Cafe

Page	NLC Code	Location Description	Location 0-99
242	**b**	**b**eing built	**D**isneyLand

For page **242** (the first number from **LOCATIONS 0-999** that does not have a workable Locational acronym) you might picture **D**isneyLand **b**eing built

Page	NLC Code	Location Description	Location 0-99
707	**q**	**q**ueue	Ghetto

And for page **707**, a long **q**ueue or **q**ueues, perhaps stretching around corners, in a **G**hetto.

GENERATING LOCATIONS 1000-9999

Probably needed very infrequently. I would suggest using as first choice the **Associated Letters/Location Description** table from **GENERATING YOUR OWN LOCATIONS 100-999** for the first of the four digits followed by the appropriate location from **LOCATIONS 0-999** for the remaining three.

Page	NLC Code	Location Description	Location 0-999
3003	**w**	**w**indy	**K**itchen

Thus, for page **3003**, a **w**indy **k**itchen, perhaps from a high one outside or a slightly ajar window or door

Page	NLC Code	Location Description	Location 0-999
6668	**p**	**p**olluted	
	s	**s**now	Secure Storage Room

For page **6668**, **s**now - perhaps tainted with aerial **p**ollution - heard gathering outside a **S**ecure **S**torage **R**oom, perhaps discernible in a lower area temperature

And for page **8046**, **r**ain upon a Department Store and perhaps a **r**ainbow high overhead.

OBJECTS 0-99

0

Table	Table Tennis	Table-mat
Tablespoon	Tarantula	Tardis
Target	Tarmac	Tarot
Tarpaulin	Taser	Teaspoon
Teleport	Teleprinter	Telescope
Telescreen	Thermite	Thermometer
Thermostat	Thimble	Thong
Ticket	Tissue	Toaster
Toboggan	Toothpaste	Tortoise
Tot	Toupe	Tracks
Tracksuit	Tractor	Trash
Treats	Trench	Trolley
Trophy	Trough	Trunk
Tumbleweed	Tunnel	Turbine
Turbo	Turnstile	Turntable
Turret	Tweezers	

1

Accordion	Aerial	Aerosol	Airlock
Aisle	Alcove	Alley	
Alligator	Antenna	Antlers	
Aquarium	Arrowslit (resembles a ⟍)		
Ashtray	toffee Apple	Umbrella	Upload

2

Balcony	Bale	Banjo	Banner
Basin	Basket	Beaker	Beams
Bell	Bench	Bike	Bikini
Blackboard	Blanket	Blender	Blinds
Booth	Bottle	Breeze	Brush
Bucket	Bullworker	Bulkhead	Bust
Buzzer	Lampshade	Landing	Lassoo
Latch	Leash	Ledge	Lock
Locker	oBelisk		
observation Blister		oBstable	
oil Lamp	(Ouija) Board	tooL	
tool Box	TV	Vault	
Vidcom	Vine	Vortex	

3

Calculator	Camouflage	Candelabra	
Capsule	Carpet	Cauldron	Cavity

Ceiling	Cenotaph	Chair	
Chandelier	Checkbook	(treasure) Chest	
Chimney	Chipboard	Cinders	Cistern
Clamp	Cliff	Clippers	Closet
Cloth	Cloud	Cobwebs	
Column	Comb	Container	Corner
Corridor	Couch	Counter	Cover
Crack	Crate	Crib	
Crowbar	Crumbs	Cubicle	
Cupboard	Cutlery	Kerb	Kettle
Keyhole	Kiosk	Klaxon	
Knickers	Magazine	Magnet	
Manhole	Manual	Marble	Medkit
Megaphone	Menu	Metronome	
Microphone	Microscope	Mist	
Mistletoe	Mittens	Modem	
Monitor	Muesli	OK	
one-way Mirror	open Window	tiled Wall	
time Clock	toM	toW	
Tower Crane (outside)		Trade Mark	
treasure Chest	trip Wire	Tug of War	
two-way Mirror	Walkway	Wall	Wallet
Wallpaper	Wardrobe	Waterbed	Well
Wheelbarrow	Wheelchair	Wristwatch	

4	Dais	Decoy	Desk	
	Detergent	Diaper	Dishwasher	Ditch
	Doll	Door	Drain	Drapes
	Draught	Drawers	Drier	Dust
	Duvet	oX	tOD	
	ticket Dispenser	towel Dispenser	(trap) Door	

5	Elevator	Enclosure	Envelope	Eraser
	Escalator	Exoskeleton	Espresso	toE
	toY			

6	Faucet	Fault	Fence	Filofax
	Fingerprints	Fireplace	Firewall	Flag
	Flagpole	Flare	Floor	
	Floorboards	Floodlights	Flowers	Flume
	Flyover (visible - or audible - near location)			
	Footbridge	Fountain	Font	Frisbee
	oS [(French) bone]			
	overhead Storage (condiments, grain etc.)			Packet
	Padlock	Pager	Paint	Pane
	Parachute	Parapet	Parcel	
	Parchment	Partition	Passport	
	Paternoster	Payslip	Pencil	

Pedestal	Pelt	Photocopier	Picture
Pigeon	Pillar	Pillow	Piping
Piston	Plate	Platform	
Plexiglass	Pliers	Point	Poker
Portal	Porthole	Postcard	Poster
Pram	Pulley	Purse	Safe
Sample	Sash	Sauna	
Scanner	Scarecrow	Scissors	Scroll
Sculpture	Sentinel	Shadows	
Sheet	Shoes	Shuriken	
Siding	Sieve	Silhouette	Sill
Sink	Skeleton	Skylight	
Slippers	Slope	Sludge	
Smorgasbord	Soap	Sofa	
Sparkler	Speedboat	Sponge	Spray
Stack	Stairlift	Stairwell	
Stake	Stalactites	Stalagmites	Stash
Statue	Steadicam	Sticker	
Stirrups	Stocking	Stool	Stove
String	Stump	Suitcase	
Suitcase	Sunbed	Support	Sword
toP	touch Screen	train Set	
tray Slide			

7

Gallery	Gangway	Gantry	Ghost
Gibbet	Gloves	Glue	Gnome
Gong	Goggles	Graffiti	Grate
Gridiron	Grotto	Guardrail	Guff
Gurney	Gust	Gutter	Jacuzzi
Jukebox	Jumpsuit	(glass of) OJ	
one-way Glass	Quicksand	Quill	toG
two-way Glass			

8

Hammock	Handbag	Handkerchief	
Handrail	Hatch	Hearth	Hedge
Hide	Hinge	Holdall	Hole
Holster	Horn	Hose	Husk
Radiator	Radio	Rafters	
Railings	Rainbow	Ramp	
Refrigerator	Reflection	Reflectors	
Registered TM	Roadside	Robot	Roll
Roof	Rope	Rotors	
Rucksack	Rune	toilet Roll	tootH

toR (rock outcrop formed by weathering, usually found on or near the summit of a hill)

9

I	I-shaped slit	Incubator	Inhaler
Intercom	Interface	Napkin	

Napsack	Nintendo	Noose	Notch
Nozzle	oN button	toN	

10 Access Opening Advanced Technology Assisted Opener
oAT oUT
TAO [(Chinese) way, path, route] tAT
toUt tUT User Terminal

11 AA batteries AA phone Analog-to-Analog
(double tape deck)

12 Acoustical Beacon Address Book Air Bag
Air Leak Air Valve Air Vent
Alarm Bell Artificial Limb Atomic Bomb
tAB totAL tUB
UltraViolet UpLoad

13 Access Card Acoustic Coupler (an interface device for coupling electrical signals by acoustic means - usually into and out of a telephone instrument; a terminal device used to link ATA terminals and radio sets with the telephone network. The link is achieved through acoustic sound signals rather than through direct electrical connection)
Actress' Mirror Air Compressor
Airing Cupboard AK (assault rifle)
Alarm Clock Answering Machine
Arc Welder Arm Chair A3
Attache Case oAK
tAM [(Scottish) woollen cap] tUM

14 Access Denied Accidental Damage A4
Automatic Doors AX tAD
tAX toAD tUX

15 A5 Air Entry American Eagle
Art Easel

16 Access Point Aerial Socket Air Sealed
Air Shaft oAF OAP
tAP Underground Passage UP
Urine Sample US

17 Access Gateway Acid Gas Acoustic Guitar
All Grain (home brewing) Apple Juice Arcade Game
tAG UnderGrowth

18 AH! Air Holes Air Rifle
Angel Hair ARoma Artificial Respirator

	Assault Rifle	oAR	tAR
	Underfloor Heating		UH!

19 Active Ingredient   Analog Input
Artificial Intelligence   tAN

20 Bird Table   Blow Torch   Body Odour
Booby Trap   Box Office   BurnOut
Lap Top   LO!

21 BA (eternal soul in Egyptian mythology; degree)
Body Armor   Breathing Air   Breathing Apparatus
Burglary Alarm   BUshel   Lost Animal
Ventilating Unit   Visual Aid   VU (view)
Vulnerable Area

22 Back Lighting   Ball Bearings   Baseball Bat
Beach Ball   Bean Bag   Black Box
Blue Velvet   Breeze Blocks   Bubble Bath
Bucking Bronco   Bulletproof Vest   Bunk Beds
Laser Beam   Laundry Basket   Leather Belt
Leather Boots   toLL   Venetian Blinds

23 Bar Code   Barbed Wire   Bathing Costume
Battery Charger   Bird Cage   Book Case
Broken Window   Broom Cupboard
Bubble Wrap   Business Card   Land Mine
Landing Module   Laundry Cart   Laundry Chute
Lawn Mower   Luggage Compartment
Vacuum Cleaner   Virtual Keyboard
Voight-Kampff (replicant detection machine)

24 Back Door   Bank Draft   Blast Door
BounDary   BunDle   Laser Disc
Lighting Dimmer an oLD person
outward Backward Downward (path of the facial nerve in the
facial canal)   Voodoo Doll

25 BE (to exist)   Bevel End   Bill of
Exchange   Binding Energy   Bucket Elevator
Low Explosive (e.g. a cracker, fireworks)   oLE!
Venom Extract   Vernal Equinox

26 Banana Peel   Bar Stool   Barge Pole
Book Shelf   Bug Sweep   Ladder Shaft
Lamp Post   Laser Printer   Lazy Susan
License Plate   Light Fixture   Light Switch
Lighting Strip   Line Feed   Liquid Pitcher

Lock Pick   Loud Speaker   **LP**
Vacuum Flask   Ventilation Shaft
Video Phone   Video Projector

27   Bass Guitar   Broken Glass   Bulletproof Glass
         Bungee Jump   Latex Gloves   Leather Gloves
         Leather Jacket   Life Jacket   Velvet Gown

28   Basketball Hoop   Bee Hive   BoreHole
         BRanch   Bullet Hole   Burn Ring
         Loud Hailer   Luggage Rack   Vehicle Rails
         Voice Recognition

29   Bank Note   Black Iron (non-stick frying pan)
         Bodily Injury   Butterfly Net
         Lethal Injection   oBI [African sorcery (obeah); to bewitch]

30   Cable Tray   Chattering Teeth   CheckOut
         Chimney Tray   Chocolate Orange   Christmas Tree
         Knock Out   Man Trap
         Microwave Oven   MOuse
         Mouse Trap   Walkie Talkie   Water Tower
         WaterTight   WeighT   Wind Tunnel
         Wind Turbine   Writing Tablet

31   CAble   Calibration Unit   Control Access
         KA (Egyptian spiritual self)   Kool Aid
         MA   Magic User   Make-Up
         Work Unit

32   Camping Bed   Candle Light   Cardboard Box
         Carrier Bag   Cat Litter   **CB**
         Ceiling Beam   Check Book   Chess Board
         Chopping Board   Christmas Lights   Cigar/-ette Box
         Cigar/-ette Lighter   Circuit Board
         Colostomy Bag   Comic Book   Contact Lenses
         Conveyor Belt   Corner Bath   Crash Barrier
         Crystal Ball   Cutlery Box   KeyBoard
         Mail Box   Marble Bag   Music Box
         oWL   toMB   Wall Bed
         Warning Light   Washing Line   Water Bottle
         Water Leak   Water Vane   Water Vapour
         Weights Bench   Whirlpool Bath   Wicker Basket
         Window Lock   Wipe Board   Wooden Bench

33   Cable Car   Cake Mixer   Call Caddy
         Calling Card   Car Wash   Carry Case
         Cash Machine   Ceiling Chains

Change Machine Cheese Wire
Children's Mobile
Circular Window Climbing Wall
Closed Window Coffee Maker Compact Mirror
Conference Call Cotton Wool Cracked Mirror
Cracked Window Credit Card Cruise Missile
Kitchen Knife Magic Carpet Magic Marker
Magic Mouth Magic Wand Meat Cleaver
Medicine Cabinet Milk Carton
Mine Cart Mirrored Cabinet Wall Chair
Wall Clock Water Wheel Watering Can
WC Weights Machine
Welding Machine Welding Mask
Wheel Clamp Whoopee Cushion Wind Chimes
Window Wiper Wire Clippers Wire Mesh

34 Cassette Deck CD CD product key
Clothes Dummy Cold Draft Cooling Duct
Kettle Drums Metal Detector Milk Duds
Mixing Desk

35 Camera Eye Cat's Eyes C5
Chest Expansion CopY
Corridor Entrance K-Y Jelly ME
toKE (drag, puff) toME WE

36 Camera Flash Card Slot Card Swipe
Cattle Prod Ceiling Fan Ceiling Sprinklers
Christmas Stocking Circular Saw
Climbing Frame Clothes Pegs Clothing Press
Coin Socket Cold Spot Concrete Stairwell
Coral Shell Cord Pull Corn Flakes
Crawl Space Cryogenic Freeze
Custard Pie Key Pad Mail Slot
Medicine Pack Mike Stand Mine Shaft
Mobile Phone Motion Sensor TCP
Walking Stick Wall Panel Wall Safe
Wanted! Poster Water Fountain Water Pipe
Water Pistol Water Slide Water Sprinkler
Weighing Scales White Satin Wood Pile
Wood Shavings Work Surface

37 Cable Jack Card Game Cattle Grid
Cheese Grater Chewing Gum OMG!
Water Jet

38 Cash Register Central Heating CHain
Chapter House Cleaning Rag Climbing Hold

Climbing Rope   Clothes Horse   Clothing   Hook
Clothing Rail   Coat Hangers
Combine Harvester   Conductor   Rail
Crash Helmet   Cubby   Hole
Curtain Hooks   Curtain Rail   Magazine   Rack
Meat Hooks   Memory Hole [any mechanism for the
disappearance or destruction   of   inconvenient   or
embarrassing material or digital records, usually in an
attempt to give the impression that something never
happened. The concept was first popularized in the George
Orwell novel *Nineteen Eighty-Four* (1949) where such
documents are immolated behind a hinged   metal   grid   in
office walls]   Metal   Rungs
Microfiche Reader   Mouse   Hole
OCH!   Water Heater   Wendy House

39   Card Input   Cast Iron   Credit Note
K-9 (Dr Who's robot dog)
KI [vital life-sustaining energy force (qi)]   oWN
White Noise   Wrought Iron

40   Dead Terminal   DeskTop   Digital Output
Disused Toilet   DO   Duct Tape
oDO   oXO

41   Damaged Article   Dead Animal   Disposal Unit
District Attorney
XU (Vietnamese monetary unit: one hundredth of a dong)

42   Dart Board   Desk Bell   Deposit Box
Diving Bell   Dog Basket   Door Bars
Door Bell   Door Lock   DownLoad
Draining Board   Dry Bulb

43   Deck Chair   Decompression Chamber
Dictation Machine   Digital Camera
Directional Microphone
Distorting Mirror
Ditch Crossing (pipeline route: usually visible by uneven
ground beneath which it runs)
Door Mat   Drain Cover
Drawers Chest   Dress Circle
Drinks Cabinet   Drinks Machine
Drum Kit   Dumb Waiter

44   Daily Diary   Disk Drive   Double Doors
Drinks Dispenser
oDD (in golf, an additional or allowed stroke)

45   Data Entry   Dead End
oDE (lyric poem addressed to someone or something)
oXY (containing oxygen)
toDY (a small West Indian insectivorous bird)

46

Damp Patch	Dance Floor	Death Slide
Deep Freeze	Digital Pen	Digital Photo
Digital Projector	Door Stop	Double Seat
Drain Piping	Draw String	Drop Siding
Dust Pan	Duty Station	
4Side (perimeter of a square)		

47

Dangerous Goods	Door Jamb
Double Glazing	Drill Jig

48

Dental Hygiene	Direct Hit	Diving Hole
Door Handle	Door Release	
Drinking Helmet	Dung Heap	

49   Delivery Note   Digital Input   Drill Instructor

50   E.T.   Ear Trumpet   Electric Toothbrush
Electronic Table toYO (a smooth straw for making hats)
YO!

51   tEA (breakfast and other flavours) Yard Arm

52

Elastic Bands	Electronic Board
Electric Boiler	Embalmed Body
Emergency Button	Emergency Lighting
Exercise Bike	Explosive Bolts

53

Electric Closet   Electric Compass   Electric Whisk
Electric Window Electrical Circuit
Electrical Contacts
Electricity Meter Exploding Cigar   Extendible Wire
tEW (rope or chain for towing a boat)   totEM
Year Calendar

54   Electric Door   EX   External Drive
tED (bear; to spread for drying)

55   Easter Egg   Emergency Exit   tEE
tYE (to wash ore in a ship; chain on a ship)

56

Ear Spoon	Ejector Seat	Electric Fan
Electric Fence	Electric Fire	Electric Shower

Electrical Fault Electrical Field Environmental Suit
Exit Sign Extractor Fan
tEF (an Ethiopian cereal grass)

57 E.G. Electric Gate Electric Guitar
Electrified Grid Emergency Generator Exercise Guide
tYG (an old drinking cup with two or more handles)

58 EH? Electric Heater Electric Razor
Extractor Hood ottER

59 Electronic Notebook tEN [(Latin) stretch; hold]

60 False Teeth Fibre Optic Fish Tank
Palm Tree Picnic Table Pipe Opening
Pump Trolley Septic Tank Slide-Out
Sliding Tray Snake Tank Socket Outlet
Sticky Tape Storage Tank Swimming Trunks
Swing Tennis toPO (mole)

61 PA Photo Album Power Adaptor
Proscenium Arch Public Announcement Security Alarm
ZA (pizza) toFU [(Japanese) a soft Oriental cheese
made from soybean milk]

62 Feed Bag Fire Blanket Flickering Light
Flood Lighting Foam Bath Foot Bath
Fork Lift Fruit Bowl Painted Lines
PaperBack Party Balloons Pedal Bin
Phone Book Phone Booth Pilot Light
Pipe Bomb Plastic Bowl Polystyrene Blocks
Polythene Bag Power Line Production Line
Pull-Up Bar Punch Bowl Sad Lamp
Safety Barrier Salad Bowl Sample Bag
Scrap Book Security Bars Shampoo Bottle
Shopping List Shutter Blinds Side Lighting
Skirting Board Sleeping Bag Soccer Ball
Scrubbing Brush Smoke Bomb Snuff Box
Speeder Bike Spilled Liquid Spot Light (-ting)
Squirt Bottle Static Line Step Ladder
Stink Bomb Street Light Strip Light
Strobe Light Stuffed Bird Sugar Bowl
Sugar Lumps Surgical Lamp Sweat Lodge

63 False Wall Filing Cabinet Film Can
Filter Coffee French Windows Paper Clips
Paper Weight Pay Meter PC
People Mover Pinball Machine Pine Cones

Plastic Curtain   Playing Cards   Press Kit
Pull Cord   Pulley Cable   Seat Cover
Secret Chamber   Secret Compartment
Security Camera   Sewing Machine   Short Circuit
Shower Cubicle   Shower Curtain   Shrink Wrap
Sleeping Capsule Slot Machine   Snap Case
Solar Wind   Spray Can   Stanley Knife
Submarine Cable   Suction Cup   Swiss Clock
Swivel Chair

64   Feather Duster   Fire Door
Flash Drive (typical USB mass-storage device)
Power Drill   Pull Down   Satellite Dish
Saw Dust   Secret Door   Security Door
Sliding Doors   Smoke Detector   Soap Dispenser
Sterile Dressing   Swing Doors

65   Fire Escape   Fire Extinguisher   Flat Escalator
ooZE   Plastic Explosive   Service Elevator
Stairwell Entrance
toPE (to drink; a kind of shark)

66   Fanny Pack   Fireman's Pole   Flare Stack
Flash Stick   Floor Panel   Floor Pedal
Floor Safe   Flyover Pillars   Folding Screen
Foot Pedal   Foot Pump   Fountain Pen
Fridge Freezer   oFF (button)   Paper File
Plow Steel   Police Siren   Pressure Panel
Pressure Point   Projection Screen   Pull String
Scrap Paper   Secret Passage   Shaving Foam
Shaving Socket   Sliding Staircase   Solar Panel
Spiral Staircase toFF   toSS

67   Flare Gun   Frosted Glass
PG certificate/Tips (tea bags)   Shallow Grave
ShotGun   Sliding Glass   Smoking Jacket
Stained Glass   Sterile Gauze   Stun Gun
Suction Grip   Super Glue

68   Fire Hose   Fire Hydrant   Fishing Hole
Fishing Rod   Floating Robot   French Horn
Panty Hose   Pen Holder   Plug Hole
Scope Rifle   Sun Roof
toPH (a rock made of fine volcanic detritus)
toSH (nonsense; neat, trim)

69   PI   Pipe Network (delivers sealed tubes
containing messages, work etc. via air pressure; in-and

outpipes at each station) Promissory Note
Serial Number Shower Nozzle
to**PI** [antelope species of the genus *Damaliscus*; (Hindi) a tropical pith helmet]

70   Game Over Glass (vacuum) Tube **GO!**
         Grand Organ Q-Tips

71   G**A**uge to**GA**

72   Gas Boiler Gas Leak Genie Bottle
         Ghetto Blaster Gift Box
         GigaByte/bit (= 1024 megabytes = 1.024m bytes)
         Globe Light Goldfish Bowl Jack in the Box
         Jewellery Box

73   Garbage Can Gas Canister Gas Meter
         Geiger Counter Golf Cart Golf Club
         Grandfather Clock

74   Glucose Drink Graph Drawing Graphic Design
         Guide Dog(s) Jack Daniel's

75   Graphic Equalizer Ground Elevation
         G**Y**roscope

76   Games Site Garden Shears Garden Sprinkler
         Gas Fire Gas Pipe Glass Screen
         Glass Sculpture Goal Post Grand Piano
         Guide Star

77   Glass Jar Golden Globe Golden Glow
         Grapefruit Juice Ground-to-Ground (missile)
         Jungle Gym

78   Garden Hose Goods Receipt Grappling Hook
         Growth Hormone Guard Rail
         Gun Rack

79   General Notes Graphic Novel
         QI (vital life-sustaining energy force)

80   HandOut Hedge Trimmer **HO!** Holding Tank
         Hot Tub o**RT** (tidbit) Remote Terminal
         Rotating Tunnel

81   **HA!**
         Home Automation (residential housing controls)

RA (ancient Egyptian sun god)   Red Alert
Remote Access   Replaceable Unit
Robot Arm

82   HandBook   Hanging Lantern(s)   HardBound
          H-Bomb   oRB   Ray-Bans
          Rocket Launcher Rotating Bed   Rubber Bullet

83   Hair Curlers   Hamster Wheel   Hand Cart
          Hanging Chains Hanging Chair
          Heavy Crane (outside)   High Chair
          Hockey Mask   oRC [marine mammal (orca), a killer
                                whale]   Railed Curtain
          Remote Control Repair Kit   Retaining Wall
          Revolving Mirror   Rock Crusher
          Room Card   Round Window
          Rowing Machine Rubber Curtains   Rubik's Cube
          Running Machine
          toRC (a necklace or armband in the form of a twisted metal
          band)

84   Hair Dryer   Hand Drier   Hard Drive
          oRD (a point, e.g. of a weapon)   Revolving Doors
          RX (receiver)

85   Hallway Entrance   Heat Exchanger
          Hoop Earrings   toRE (a surface described by
          rotation of conic section about a line)
          toRY   tRY

86   Hard File   Head Phones   Helter Skelter   Hi-Fi
          Hiding Place   Hole Punch   Hot Spot
          HP Sauce   Hypersleep Freezer
          oRS (heraldic color gold)   Rat Poison
          Record Player   Removable Panel
          Retina Scan   Rice Screen   Road Sign
          Roller Skates   Rubber Plant

87   Hair Grips   Harpoon Gun   Head Gear
          HemoGlobin/HaemoGlobin (the iron-containing oxygen-
          transport metallo-protein in the red blood cells and tissues of
          some invertebrates. HaemoGlobin in the blood transports
          oxygen from the lungs or gills to the rest of the bodily tissues
          where it releases the oxygen for cell use)
          Holy Grail   Rubber Gloves

88   Hand-Held   Hand Holds   Hard Hat
          Hi-Hat (cymbal) Hidden Room   Hula Hoop

Rabbit Hutch   Rocking Horse   Russian Roulette

89   **HI!**   to**RI** [(pl.) torus: large convex mouldings]
t**RI** [(L; G) three]

90   I/O (Input/Output)   Ice Tray   Insect Tank
IT   **NO!**   No Trespassing
o**NO** (large mackerel)   oo**NT** [(Hindi) a camel]
t**IT** (small bird)   **TNT**

91   **IA** [(L) names of classes or places]   In Utero
Internet Access   Intruder Alert!
NU [(French) nude; perhaps a posing model]

92   Ice Box   Instructions Book   Invisible Barrier
Iron Bar   Ironing Board   Neon Light
Nodding Bird (plastic)   Note Book
Notice Board   o**IL**
t**IL** (sesame plant)   to**IL**

93   Infinity Mirrors   Internal Mail
Integrated Circuit [(also known as *microcircuit*, *micro* or
silicon chip) a miniaturized electronic circuit (consisting
mainly of semiconductor devices, as well as passive
components) manufactured in the surface of a thin substrate
of semiconductor material. Made possible by the low
production costs, Integrated Circuits are used in almost all
modern electronic equipment]
Net Curtains   Nut Cracker   Nylon Curtains
o**IK**   t**IC**

94   **ID** [**ID**entification; (Freud) unorganised part of the
personality structure containing the basic drives; (L) a
quality]   Inflatable Dinghy
Internal Document   Interface Device
o**ID** [(G) resembling]

95   No Entry   No Exit   o**NE**   t**IE**
to**NE**

96   **IF, IS** Ink Pad   Ink Printer   Instant Pudding
i**P**od   t**IP**

97   Installation Guide   Intelligence Quotient
Natural Gas   t**IG**

98   InfraRed   Iron Railings   Natural Rubber

~ 160 ~

It may well be noted that using this system literally only permits one use of each Object at each Location when of course in reality there are often several identical Objects at each. In this case, and to even make Location preparation simpler, you could use **C**upboard **1** for Object **31**, **C**upboard **2** for Object **32**, **C**upboard **3** for Object **33**, and so on.

ALTERNATIVE LOCATIONS AND OBJECTS TO MY SUGGESTIONS

* acronyms, such as those used in IT, from such finders on the Net
* airport codes doubling for the Location they represent
* brainstorm Locations and Objects with friends and colleagues
* classroom numbers: classroom **C1**, for instance, could be Location number **31**, **C2 32** etc.; similarly for, say **3** Corridors
* company or brand names and products such as **43 TDK**, Britvic **55**, Levi **501**
* dramatic or emergency (though probably not tragic) occurrences associated with certain Locations and Objects
* elements of the periodic table would best be learned by associating each atomic number with a Location to preserve its order but you could, if you are not using a memory palace to memorise them, use their symbol as an Object or even Location number. Thus Gold, whose atomic number is 79, could be used, as its symbol is **Au** when most memorable to you as Object number **11**
* erotic Locations, situations or Objects
* *Every Good Boy Deserves Fudge The Book of Mnemonic Devices* by Rod L. Evans, Ph.D. (Penguin, 2007)
* favourite foods or brands
* favourite gadgets or toys
* fictional or documentary Locations or maps from your favourite films, novels, role-playing or video games, still images and photographs, even musically-evoked landscapes etc. or their titles
* Greek and Latin roots in English (full list should be easily available on the Web; a more limited one in: *Master Your Memory* (David and Charles, 1989) by Tony Buzan
* guides to the known universe
* historical or fictional dates: if you know historical events from, say, BC or AD 594, you could use those for room 594 or if an important anniversary is on 1 December, you could

use that for room 112
* house, room or street number or other numbers of personal resonance (examples: my room number during my first year at University, **M29**, could be used for Location **329**; a house **21A** for **211** and Apartment **7L** for **72**)
* improvising Objects appropriate to each Location
* initials of a familiar martial art as Location, taking place among the Objects
* initials of favourite vehicles, street names or sports teams
* keep notes of people or things you find most interesting, which are those that tend to stick in your long-term memory, and use those in your system
* license plates or other numbers on familiar vehicles representing the vehicle itself
* local, area and international codes
* Locations or situations from dreams that match or suggest or fit a Location number
* page number itself which, in being excluded may become more memorable
* people's and pet's initials
* piles of money totalling an amount then used as your number
* pop group names such as **520 ELO** or those easily turned into acronyms, such as **798 G'N'R**
* product or serial numbers
* rooms in yours or friends' houses
* rooms or Objects shaped like letters, numbers or their combinations
* score-lines or numerical facts associated with favourite sports matches. One of the most exciting soccer games, for me, was Brazil beating Argentina 3-1 in the 1982 World Cup so I may use memories of the facts and visceral feelings I associate with that game when needing to use the number 31 as a temporary location on a problem at work
* store or chain abbreviations
* street numbers (could cover several rooms) of places you know or like, perhaps using all the house numbers in your street if you know them so well
* times of the day (if your memory and perception are so accurate)
* using, as long as there is no confusion, items from the **LOCATIONS 0-999** as Objects or even vice-versa, if this works for you
* world or bodily maps
* zip or post codes

It may well be noted that using this system literally only permits one use of each Location per page number when you may wish to use several Locations with the same name. I would suggest, for instance, to use more than one **2 B**edroom in your Palace, you could use Bedroom **1** for Location **21, B**edroom **2** for Location **22,** Bedroom **3** for Location **23**, and so on.

And maybe keep a copy of this book on your person so you can jot in new Locations and Objects as they occur to you.

10 SAMPLE LOCATIONS AND OBJECTS

Most of these Locations and Objects are easy to visualise from your memories and fantasies of similar such.

Memory champions usually have thoroughly memorized up about 40 "journeys" each consisting of 50 stages (probably 50 for memorizing packs of cards without Jokers; for competition (please see **MEMORY IMPROVEMENT TOPICS A-Z** for links to my preferred methods of memorising sequences of playing cards).

Bruno Furst, my Number-Letter Code to whose outlined in his book *The Practical Way To A Better Memory* (R. & W. Heap, 1977) I find far more user-friendly, is claimed on the dust jacket by the *Daily Mail* newspaper to have: "committed 200 of the world's best books to memory". The best way I can suggest of achieving that is to have the same number of Locations as the book of these with the most pages, the Locations and Objects being devised during reading, then follow my suggestions in the section **CONTINUING TO USE THE SAME LOCATIONS AND EVEN OBJECTS FOR FURTHER TEXTS.**

You could, if it saves you time, transplant each or most of each standard list of Objects from any of these Locations to other Locations you may need to use but I have populated each one with objects likely to be found - and therefore most memorable - in each one:

1 AIRPORT

1 Ashtray	**2** TV
3 Window	**4** Desk
5 Elevator	**6** Faucet
7 Grill (behind breakfast bar)	**8** Handrail

9 Napsack

10 Access Opening (to electrical wiring)

11 AA phone

12 Air Vent

13 Acoustic Coupler (security office)

14 Automatic Doors

15 Air Entry

16 Access Point

17 tAG (on luggage)

18 tAR (on runway)

19 tAN (on tourist)

20 Body Odor (emanating from user of) Lap Top

21 Breathing Apparatus (next to medical passenger)

22 Boarding Lounge

23 Baggage Collection

24 an oLD person

25 BE

26 Bar Stool before Lazy Susan (Chinese restaurant)

27 Bass Guitar

28 Vehicle Rails (airport train)

29 Black Iron (restaurant)

30 Walkie Talkie

31 Make-Up

32 Carrier Bag

33 WC Window Wiper

34 CD

35 Corridor Entrance

36 Coin Socket

37 Cheese Grater (in restaurant)

38 Magazine Rack (boarding area bookshop)

39 Check-In

40 oXO

41 XU

42 Door Bell

43 Door Knob

44 oDD (sight or in arcade golf game)

45 Data Entry

46 Digital Pen

47 Dangerous Goods

48 Dental Hygiene (wealthy passengers' teeth)

49 Delivery Note

50 toYO

51 (breakfast) tEA

52 Elastic Bands

53 Electricity Meter

54 External Drive

55 tEE (golf game in video arcade) **56** Electrical Fault

57 tYG

58 Extractor Hood (restaurant)

59 tEN

60 Sticky Tape

61 ZA

62 Fork Lift   Phone Booth

63 Playing Cards (played by waiting passengers)

64 Smoke Detector

65 Fire Extinguisher Stairwell Entrance

66 Flash Stick (passenger laptop)

67 Super Glue

68 to**PH**

69 Serial Number

70 GO!

71 to**GA**

72 Gift Box

73 Garbage Can

74 Guide Dogs

75 Ground Elevation

76 Goal Post (video arcade soccer game)

77 Golden Globe

78 Guard Rail

79 General Notes

80 o**RT**

81 RA

82 Hard**B**ound

83 Hair Curlers

84 o**RD**

85 Hoop Earrings (on sexy young passenger)

86 Head Phones

87 Head Gear

88 Hand-Held

89 HI!

90 o**NO** (large mackerel) smell from fish-serving restaurant

91 Internet Access

92 Neon Light

93 Integrated Circuit   t**IC**

94 Internal Document

95 t**IE** (on embarking pilot)

96 t**IP**

97 t**IG**	**98** **N**atural **R**ubber
99 t**IN**	**0** Table

2 **B**EDROOM

1 Umbrella	**2** ouija **B**oard TV
3 Closet	**4** **D**oor
5 to**Y**	**6** **F**loor
7 Gloves	**8** **R**adiator
9 o**N**	**10** **A**ccess **O**pening (to insulation area)
11 **A**nalog-to-**A**nalog	**12** **A**ir **V**ent
13 **A**ctress' Mirror	**14** **A**4
15 **A**ir Entry	**16** **A**ccess Point **A**erial Socket
17 t**AG** (price ~; on new shirt)	**18** t**AR**
19 t**AN**	**20** Lap Top
21 **BA**	**22** Leather **B**elt
23 **B**ook Case	**24** o**LD**
25 **B**evel End	**26** Light **S**witch

27 Bungee Jump

28 BoreHole

29 Black Iron

30 Cable

31 CAble

32 Chess Board

33 Children's Mobile

34 CD

35 Corridor Entrance

36 Wall Safe

37 Cable Jack

38 Clothing Rail

39 Cast Iron

40 Digital Output

41 Dead Animal (budgie on bottom of cage)

42 Door Lock

43 Door Knob

44 Disk Drive

45 oDE

46 Drain Piping

47 Double Glazing

48 Door Handle

49 Delivery Note

50 E.T.

51 (breakfast) tEA

52 Elastic Bands

53 Extendible Wire

54 External Drive

55 tEE

56 Electrical Fault

57 Electric Guitar

58 Electric Heater	**59** Electronic Notebook
60 Sticky Tape	**61** Power Adaptor
62 Pull-Up Bar (top of doorway)	**63** Paper Clips
64 Feather Duster	**65** ooZE
66 Folding Screen Scrap Paper	**67** Super Glue
68 toPH	**69** Serial Number
70 GO!	**71** toGA
72 Jewellery Box	**73** Grandfather Clock
74 Graphic Design	**75** Ground Elevation
76 Garden Shears	**77** Golden Globe
78 Goods Receipt	**79** General Notes
80 Hot Tub	**81** Home Automation
82 HandBook	**83** Remote Control
84 Hair Dryer	**85** Hoop Earrings
86 Head Phones	**87** Hair Grips
88 Hand-Held	**89** toRI

90 I/O (Input/Output)   **91** Internet Access

92 Neon Light   **93** Integrated Circuit

94 ID   **95** tIE

96 Ink Printer   **97** Intelligence Quotient

98 Natural Rubber   **99** a tIN

0 Table

3 CELLAR

1 Alcove   **2** Bottle (matured, un-drunk wine in dusty ~)

3 Cobwebs   Well   **4** (trap) Door

5 toE   **6** Silhouette

7 Jukebox   **8** Handrail

9 Napsack   **10** Air Tight

11 Analog-to-Analog   **12** Air Vent   Alarm Bell

13 oAK (material of old table)   **14** toAD

15 Air Entry   **16** tAP

17 tAG   **18** tAR

19 Active Ingredient   **20** BurnOut (old electrical circuit)

21 Breathing Apparatus	**22** Ball Bearings
23 Book Case Laundry Chute	**24** oLD
25 Bevel End	**26** LP
27 Velvet Gown	**28** BoreHole
29 Black Iron	**30** Chimney TrayMan Trap
31 Control Access	**32** Ceiling Beam Water Leak
33 Mirrored Cabinet	**34** Clothes Dummy
35 toKE	**36** Walking Stick
37 Cable Jack	**38** Cubby Hole
39 Cast Iron	**40** Digital Output
41 Dead Animal (mouse)	**42** Dry Bulb
43 Deck Chair	**44** Disk Drive
45 oXY	**46** Door Stop
47 Door Jamb	**48** Door Handle
49 Delivery Note	**50** E.T.
51 (out of date) tEA	**52** Electric Boat

53 Electricity Meter	**54** t**ED**
55 t**YE**	**56** Environmental Suit
57 Emergency Generator	**58** Electric Heater
59 t**EN**	**60** to**PO**
61 Security Alarm	**62** Scrap Book Stuffed Bird
63 Film Can	**64** Power Drill
65 oo**ZES**tairwell Entrance	**66** Pull String
67 Shallow Grave	**68** to**PH**
69 Pipe Network	**70** Grand Organ
71 G**A**uge	**72** Gift Box
73 Gas Meter	**74** Graph Drawing
75 Ground Elevation	**76** Garden Shears
77 Ground-to-Ground	**78** Garden Hose
79 General Notes	**80** o**RT**
81 R**A**	**82** Rocket Launcher
83 to**RC**	**84** o**RD**

85 Hoop Earrings

86 Record Player

87 HaemoGlobin

88 Hi-Hat

89 HI!

90 tIT

91 Intruder Alert!

92 oIL

93 tIC

94 oID

95 tIE

96 tIP

97 tIG

98 Infra-red Radiation

99 a pair of I's

0 Thermostat   Trophy

yacht (resembles a **4**)

1 Ashtray

2 Ladder (between decks)

3 (water-flecked) Window

4 (trap) Door

5 toY

6 Stairwell

7 OJ

8 Radio

9 Nintendo

10 Air Tight

11 AA phone

12 Air Vent

13 Acoustic Coupler

14 A4

15 A5	**16** Access Point (telephone connection)
17 tAG	**18** oAR
19 tAN	**20** Body Odor (from hot weather)
21 Breathing Apparatus	**22** Bunk Beds
23 Business Card	**24** outward Backward Downward
25 BE	**26** Bar Stool
27 Bass Guitar	**28** Loud Hailer
29 oBI	**30** Walkie Talkie
31 CAble	**32** Window Lock
33 WC	**34** Cooling Duct
35 Corridor Entrance	**36** Medicine Pack
37 Cable Jack	**38** Cubby Hole (largely containing repair items)
39 Cast Iron	**40** Digital Output
41 XU	**42** DownLoad
43 Deck Chair	**44** oDD
45 Data Entry	**46** Door Stop

47 Double Glazing	**48** Drinking Helmet
49 Delivery Note	**50** toYO
51 (herbal) tEA	**52** Explosive Bolts
53 Extendible Wire	**54** tED
55 tYE	**56** Environmental Suit
57 Emergency Generator	**58** ottER
59 tEN	**60** Sticky Tape
61 toFU	**62** Painted Lines (for safer walking during waves)
63 Playing Cards	**64** Swing Doors
65 toPE	**66** Shaving Socket
67 Flare Gun	**68** toPH
69 Serial Number	**70** GO!
71 toGA	**72** Ghetto Blaster
73 Garbage Can	**74** Graph Drawing
75 Ground Elevation	**76** Guide Star
77 Ground-to-Ground	**78** Garden Hose

79 General Notes	**80** oRT
81 Home Automation	**82** HandBook
83 oRC	**84** RX
85 Hoop Earrings	**86** Head Phones
87 Head Gear	**88** Hand-Held
89 HI!	**90** oNO
91 Internet Access	**92** oIL
93 Integrated Circuit	**94** Interface Device
95 toNE	**96** tIP
97 tIG	**98** Infra-red Radiation
99 tIN	**0** Table

5 YARD

1 Ashtray	**2** Brush
3 tug of War	**4** (exit) Door
5 toY	**6** Flowers (between cracks)
7 Graffiti (by intruders on wall)	**8** Railings

9 Napsack	**10** Advanced Technology
11 AA phone	**12** tUB
13 oAK	**14** toAD
15 American Eagle	**16** tAP
17 Access Gateway	**18** tAR
19 tAN	**20** Body Odor
21 BA	**22** Ball Bearings
23 Barbed Wire	**24** oLD
25 Bevel End	**26** Loud Speaker
27 Velvet Gown	**28** Vehicle Rails (train-lines outside or passing over)
29 Black Iron	**30** Wind Turbine
31 CAble	**32** Weights Bench
33 WC	**34** Milk Duds
35 toKE	**36** Cold Spot
37 Cattle Grid	**38** CHain
39 Cast Iron	**40 DO**

41 District Attorney	**42** Door Lock
43 Door Knob	**44** oDD
45 toDY	**46** Death Slide
47 Dangerous Goods	**48** Dung Heap
49 Drill Instructor	**50** E.T.
51 tEA	**52** Electric Boat
53 totEM	**54** tED
55 tEE	**56** tEF
57 Emergency Generator	**58** Extractor Hood
59 Electronic Notebook	**60** toPO
61 ZA	**62** Fork Lift
63 Stanley Knife	**64** Feather Duster
65 toPE	**66** Fanny Pack
67 ShotGun	**68** toPH
69 toPI	**70** Grand Organ
71 toGA	**72** Ghetto Blaster

73 Garbage Can	**74** Guide Dogs
75 Ground Elevation	**76** Goal Post
77 Ground-to-Ground	**78** Garden Hose
79 QI	**80** Hot Tub
81 RA	**82** Rocket Launcher
83 Rowing Machine	**84 RX**
85 tRY	**86** oRS
87 Holy Grail	**88** Hi-Hat
89 HI!	**90** tIT
91 Intruder Alert!	**92** tIL
93 tIC	**94 ID**
95 oNE	**96** tIP
97 tIG	**98** Natural Rubber
99 tIN	**0** Table-mat

6 STUDY (in a country estate)

1 Antlers (part of stuffed deer-head on wall)

2 Lampshade	**3** Chair

4 Desk	**5** Eraser
6 Fireplace (huge, logged)	**7** Grill
8 Ramp	**9** Nintendo
10 Advanced Technology	**11** Analog-to-Analog
12 Air Vent	**13** Acoustic Coupler
14 tAX	**15** American Eagle
16 tAP	**17** tAG
18 tAR	**19** Active Ingredient (in packetted drink)
20 Lap Top	**21** BA
22 Laser Beam (detection system)	**23** Book Case
24 oLD	**25** Bevel End
26 Video Projector	**27** Bass Guitar
28 BoreHole	**29** Black Iron
30 Chimney Tray	**31** CAble
32 Cigarette Lighter	**33** Wall Clock
34 CD	**35** Corridor Entrance

36 Cord Pull	**37** Cable Jack
38 Memory Hole	**39** Card Input
40 o**XO**	**41** District Attorney
42 DownLoad	**43** Dictation Machine
44 o**DD**	**45** o**DE**
46 Draw String	**47** Door Jamb
48 Direct Hit	**49** Delivery Note
50 to**YO**	**51** (Earl Grey) t**EA**
52 Elastic Bands	**53** tot**EM**
54 **EX-**	**55** t**EE**
56 t**EF**	**57** t**YG**
58 Electric Heater	**59** t**EN**
60 Sticky Tape	**61** **ZA**
62 Fruit Bowl	**63** Filing Cabinet
64 Feather Duster	**65** Spiral Staircase
66 Projection Screen	**67** **PG** Tips

68 to**SH**

69 Pipe Network

70 Grand Organ

71 to**GA**

72 Jewellery Box

73 Grandfather Clock

74 Graphic Design

75 Ground Elevation

76 Games Site

77 Golden Globe

78 Growth Hormone (secured plastic bottle on desk)

79 General Notes

80 o**RT** (tidbit)

81 Home Automation

82 Hard**B**ound

83 Running Machine

84 **RX** (receiver)

85 to**RE**

86 Retina Scan

87 Holy Grail

88 Hi-**H**at

89 to**RI**

90 Ice Tray

91 Intruder Alert! (for house boundary)

92 to**IL**

93 Integrated Circuit

94 Interface Device

95 t**IE**

96 Ink Printer

97 Intelligence **Q**uotient

98 Infra-red Radiation   **99** a pair of I's (peepholes)

0 Thermostat

7 GREENHOUSE within a GARDEN area surrounded by JUNGLE

1 Ashtray   Umbrella   **2** Ladder

3 (cracked) Window   **4** (glassed, entrance) Door

5 toE (of protection boots or employee)

6 Flowers   **7** Gloves

8 Hammock   **9** Napsack

10 Air Tight (flask)   **11** AA phone

12 tUB   **13** oAK

14 toAD   **15** Air Entry

16 tAP   **17** Access Gateway (with
                                   magnetic seal)

18 oAR   **19** tAN

20 Body Odor   **21** Breathing Apparatus

22 Bunk Beds   **23** Laundry Chute

24 outward Backward Downward   **25** BE

26 Loud Speaker **27** Bungee Jump

28 Loud Hailer **29** o**BI**

30 Wind Turbines (partially powering the place)

31 KA **32** Conveyor Belt

33 Coffee Maker **34** Milk Duds

35 to**KE** **36** Climbing Frame

37 Cattle Grid **38 CH**ain below **W**ater Heater

39 Card Input **40** o**XO**

41 Dead Animal (ant-eater) **42** Door Lock

43 Deck Chair **44** o**DD**

45 to**DY** **46** Death Slide

47 Double Glazing **48** Dung Heap (tapir)

49 Delivery Note **50** to**YO**

51 (herbal) t**EA** **52** Electric Boat (plaything in bucket of water)

53 Electricity Meter   to**TEM 54** t**ED**

55 t**EE** **56** t**EF**

57 t**YG**

58 Extractor Hood (in kitchen area)

59 Electronic Notebook

60 to**PO**

61 Security Alarm

62 Sweat Lodge

63 Pull Cord

64 Swing Doors

65 oo**ZE**

66 Scrap Paper

67 ShotGun

68 to**PH**

69 to**PI**

70 GO!

71 GAuge

72 Gas Leak

73 Garbage Can

74 Graph Drawing   Guide Dog

75 Ground Elevation

76 Garden Shears Goal Post

77 Ground-to-Ground

78 Garden Hose

79 Q**I**

80 Hot Tub

81 Home Automation

82 HandBook

83 to**RC**

84 RX

85 Hoop Earrings

86 Hi-Fi

87 HaemoGlobin

88 Hand-Held

89 tRI

90 tIT

91 Intruder Alert!

92 tIL

93 tIC

94 oID

95 tIE

96 tIP

97 tIG

98 Infra-red Radiation   Natural Rubber

99 tIN

0 Thermostat

8 RESTAURANT by a RIVER

1 Ashtray

2 Blinds

3 Menu on top of Microwave

4 (revolving) Door

5 Escalator

6 Smorgasbord

7 OJ

8 tootH

9 Napsack

10 Air Tight

11 AA phone

12 tUB

13 oAK

14 Automatic Doors

15 Air Entry	**16** tAP
17 tAG	**18** oAR
19 Active Ingredient	**20** Lap Top
21 Breathing Apparatus	**22** Leather Belt
23 Bar Code	**24** an oLD person
25 BE	**26** Bar Stool
27 Bass Guitar	**28** BoreHole

29 Black Iron (non-stick frying pan)

30 Wind Turbine	**31** CAble
32 Chopping Board	**33** Coffee Maker
34 Milk Duds	**35** toKE
36 Water Fountain	**37** Cable Jack
38 Water Heater	**39** Card Input
40 oXO	**41** Dead Animal (trout in river)
42 Door Lock	**43** Dumb Waiter
44 oDD	**45** oXY

46 Death Slide (over river)

47 Double Glazing

48 Dental Hygiene

49 Drill Instructor

50 E.T.

51 tEA   (selection)

52 Electric Boat

53 totEM

54 EX

55 tEE

56 tEF

57 tYG

58 ottER

59 tEN

60 toPO

61 ZA   toFU

62 Fruit Bowl

63 Submarine Cable

64 Swing Doors

65 toPE

66 Fridge Freezer

67 PG Tips

68 toSH

69 toPI

70 GO!

71 toGA

72 Gas Leak

73 Garbage Can

74 Guide Dogs

75 Ground Elevation

76 Garden Shears

77 Golden Globe

78 Garden Hose　　　　　　**79** QI

80 oRT　　　　　　　　　**81** RA

82 HardBound　　　　　　　**83** Hair Curlers

84 Revolving Doors　　　　　**85** Hoop Earrings

86 HP Sauce　　　　　　　**87** Hair Grips

88 Hi-Hat　　　　　　　　**89** tRI

90 Ice Tray　　　　oNO　　**91** Internet Access

92 Nodding Bird (plastic)　tIL　**93** tIC

94 Internal Document　　　　**95** tONE

96 tIP　　　　　　　　　**97** Intelligence Quotient

98 Natural Rubber　　　　　**99** tIN

0 Table-mat

9 ISLAND

1 Ashtray　　　　Umbrella　　**2** Blanket

3 Well (natural, with roped bucket for collecting water)

4 Duvet　　　　　　　　　**5** toE

6 Fence (to keep nuisance animals out)

7 OJ

8 Hammock

9 Napsack

10 Air Tight

11 AA phone

12 t**AB** t**UB**

13 o**AK**

14 to**AD**

15 American Eagle

16 Acoustic Guitar

17 t**AG**

18 o**AR** t**AR**

19 t**AN**

20 Body **O**dor

21 Breathing **A**pparatus

22 Leather Belt

23 Land **M**ine (exploded remnants in sand)

24 outward **Backward Downward**

25 BE

26 LP

27 Bungee **J**ump

28 Loud Hailer

29 o**BI**

30 Wind **T**urbine

31 CAble

32 to**MB**

33 Magic **C**arpet

34 CD

35 K-Y Jelly

36 Medicine **P**ack

37 Cable **J**ack

38 Cubby Hole (under ground-drop)

39 Cast Iron

40 DO

41 Dead Animal

42 DownLoad

43 Deck Chair

44 oDD

45 toDY

46 Dressing Screen

47 Dangerous Goods

48 Drinking Helmet   Dung Heap

49 Drill Instructor

50 toYO

51 tEA   (breakfast)

52 Electric Boat

53 totEM

54 tED

55 tYE

56 Environmental Suit

57 Emergency Generator (wind-up)

58 ottER

59 tEN

60 toPO

61 toFU

62 Plastic Bowl

63 Playing Cards

64 Power Drill

65 toPE (a kind of shark)

66 Fanny Pack	**67** Super Glue
68 toPH	**69** toPI
70 GO!	**71** toGA
72 Ghetto Blaster	**73** Garbage Can
74 Graphic Design	**75** Ground Elevation
76 Goal Post (crude)	**77** Ground-to-Ground
78 Growth Hormone	**79** General Notes
80 oRT	**81** RA
82 Rocket Launcher	**83** oRC
84 oRD	**85** Hoop Earrings (prominent on sexy female swimmer)
86 Hot Spot	**87** HaemoGlobin
88 Hand-Held	**89** toRI
90 oNO tIT	**91** Internet Access
92 oIL	**93** tIC
94 ID oID	**95** oNE
96 tIP	**97** tIG

98 Natural Rubber (sap from palm tree)

99 tIN   **0** hOle

10 ADMINISTRATION OFFICE on the ATLANTIC OCEAN coast

1 Antlers (stuffed deer-head central on wall)

2 Basin Blinds   **3** (open) Window

4 Desk   **5** Eraser

6 Flag (US)   **7** Glue   OJ

8 Radiator   **9** Intercom

10 oUT   **11** AA batteries

12 Air Vent   **13** Answering Machine

14 AX   **15** American Eagle (emblem)

16 Access Point   **17** UnderGrowth (skirting office
                                            building)

18 ARoma   **19** tAN

20 Lap Top   **21** Lost Animal

22 Back Lighting Beach Ball (played with on the sand outside)

23 Battery Charger   Book Case

24 Lighting Dimmer	**25** Bill of Exchange
26 Book Shelf	**27** Life Jacket
28 Loud Hailer	**29** Bodily Injury
30 Microwave Oven	**31** Kool Aid
32 Window Lock	**33** Wall Clock **WC**
34 Cold Draft	**35** to**ME**
36 Water Fountain	**37** Cable Jack
38 Clothing Rack	**39** Card Input
40 Dead Terminal	**41** Disposal Unit
42 Door Bell	**43** Dictation Machine
44 Daily Diary	**45** Data Entry
46 Door Stop	**47** Double Glazing
48 Door Handle	**49** Delivery Note
50 to**YO**	**51** (strong breakfast) t**EA**
52 Elastic Bands	**53** Electricity Meter
54 t**ED** (bear)	**55** t**YE**

56 Exit Sign	**57** tYG
58 Electric Heater	**59** Electronic Notebook
60 Fish Tank Swing Tennis	**61** Security Alarm
62 Phone Book	**63** Security Camera
64 Smoke Detector	**65** Fire Extinguisher
66 Paper File	**67** Super Glue
68 Panty Hose	**69** Pipe Network
70 Q-Tips	**71** GAuge
72 Gift Box	**73** Garbage Can Gas Meter Grandfather Clock
74 Graph Drawing	**75** GYroscope
76 Games Site	**77** Golden Glow
78 Goods Receipt	**79** General Notes
80 HandOut	**81** Replaceable Unit
82 Hanging Lanterns	**83** Hair Curlers
84 Hand Drier	**85** tRY
86 Hot Spot	**87** Hair Grips

88 Rabbit Hutch

89 to**RI**

90 I/O (Input/Output) trays

91 Internet Access

92 Notice Board

93 Nylon Curtains

94 ID

95 t**IE**

96 Ink Printer

97 Installation Guide

98 Iron Railings

99 a pair of I's (peepholes)

0 h**O**le   Table   Table-mat
      Trash   Turnstile

Thermostat   Toothpaste
Tweezers

Different sources yield slightly different spellings

SELECTED BIBLIOGRAPHY

Tony Buzan — *Master Your Memory* (David and Charles, 1989)

Tony Buzan — *Use Your Memory* (BBC Books, 1995)

Jim Diamond and Curtis Holliman, Ph.D — *The Mnemonics Book* (Professional Press, 2009)

Harry Lorayne — *Super Memory Super Student* (Little, Brown and Company, 1990)

Dominic O'Brien — *How To Develop A Brilliant Memory Week By Week* (Duncan Baird Publishers, 2005)

MEMORY IMPROVEMENT TOPICS A-Z

Page references are for my favourite technique for each topic; I include my suggestions and recommendations in brackets. When a technique requires the *journey system* or *Roman Room*, you may of course simply use my Memory Palace technique:

*	adjectives	*Use Your Memory* 161-163
*	binary code	*A Brilliant Memory Week By Week* 45
*	capitals	*A Brilliant Memory Week By Week* 60-62
		Use Your Memory 109-112
*	computer programming [see: numbers and letters (strings of)]	
*	dates	*A Brilliant Memory Week By Week* 118-119; 138-139
		Use Your Memory 129-130
		Super Memory 87; 92-100
*	diary/planner	*Use Your Memory* 121-123
		A Brilliant Memory Week By Week 112-117
*	the dictionary	*A Brilliant Memory Week By Week* 146-148
*	diet	*A Brilliant Memory Week By Week* 155-157
*	directions	*A Brilliant Memory Week By Week* 54-57
*	dreams	*Use Your Memory* 175-176
*	faces and names	*A Brilliant Memory Week By Week* 50-53
*	facts such as the *Trivial Pursuit* game	
		A Brilliant Memory Week By Week 158-159
*	fiction/novels	*A Brilliant Memory Week By Week* 80-81
		Super Memory 160-167
*	foreign languages	*A Brilliant Memory Week By Week* 63-65
		Super Memory 56-64

(for languages dividing nouns into two genders you could divide each Location into two zones, one half for male nouns, the other for female)
* golf courses in hole order with surface, wind tendency and other details
* holiday items (would keep a copy as a mind map to not miss anything crucial)
* images and photographs   *A Brilliant Memory Week By Week* 16-17

*	jokes	*A Brilliant Memory Week By Week* 78-79
*	journey system	*A Brilliant Memory Week By Week* 32-37

(for a simpler version of memory palacing, though one lacking the numerical order prompting for each chunk of information of my NLC and **OBJECTS 0-99** system, you could use my **LOCATIONS 0-999, GENERATING YOUR OWN LOCATIONS 100-999** and **GENERATING LOCATIONS 1000-9999** for each page number to be recalled then this system outlined in Dominic's book for the information on each page to be recalled)

*	law and politics	*Super Memory* 109-114
*	mathematical, scientific and similar formula	
		Super Memory 129-159 and Phil Chambers' and my forthcoming book
*	medicine and dentistry	*Super Memory* 169-171
*	mnemonics and acronyms	*A Brilliant Memory Week By Week* 18-21
		The Mnemonics Book 213-219
*	music	*Super Memory* 124-128 167-168
*	news	*A Brilliant Memory Week By Week* 124-125
*	numbers and letters (strings of)	
		A Brilliant Memory Week By Week esp. 72-77, 98-100, 104-107; **FORTHCOMING**

(the Dominic System outlined in these pages seems to me by far the most user-friendly for memorising strings of numbers and letters and, as it uses ten of the same letter-number associations as I do in its NLC, with mine also integrating the remaining sixteen letters of the alphabet, should be the easiest for users of this book to pick up. In his published work to date, however, Dominic seems to only outline a person-action system for each paired chunk of digits; I would recommend this system be generally expanded, easily enough, to a more efficient person-action-object)

*	periodic table	*A Brilliant Memory Week By Week* 68-69
		Super Memory 126

(I would suggest using a different Location for each element and a different Object for each property OR using one Location for each category of elements and the Object number within that location to match respectively each element's atomic number)

*	phone conversations	*A Brilliant Memory Week By Week* 101-103
		Super Memory 161-164
*	phone numbers	*A Brilliant Memory Week By Week* 120-121

		Use Your Memory 117-119
*	playing cards	*A Brilliant Memory Week By Week* 108-111; 149-151; 160-161
*	quotations	*A Brilliant Memory Week By Week* 84-86
*	room full of people	*A Brilliant Memory Week By Week* 152-154

		The Mnemonics Book 89-95
		Use Your Memory 141-159

* dialogue/discussions/interviews/jokes/lecture and study notes/negotiations/poetry/presentations/reports/sales information and "procedure"/speeches

		A Brilliant Memory Week By Week 91-93; 129-131
		Use Your Memory 169-174
*	speed reading	*A Brilliant Memory Week By Week* 82-83
		The Mnemonics Book 97-103
*	test exercises	*A Brilliant Memory Week By Week* 162-169
		Use Your Memory 177-178
*	US states	*Super Memory* 172
*	vocabulary and spelling	*A Brilliant Memory Week By Week* 58-59
		Super Memory 53-55; 65-73; 101-108

METHODS MOST LIKELY TO MAKE THE MOST OF YOUR INTELLIGENCE (in roughly decreasing order of importance)

While practicing the intellectual initiatives you need for employment or study, I would also try then integrate the following into your routine:

1. Harry Kahne *The Multiple Mentality Course* (1920): short story length and presently available as free download; several exercises involve play with three- and four-letter words

2. Dual N-Back: this game, available cheaply or for free for download, seems to be the one brain training game that shows promise in the development of key aspects of fluid intelligence such as short-term memory, concentration span and discernment

3. Omega-3 Fatty Acids: easily available and rather inexpensive, ongoing research suggests daily consumption may increase intelligence and help alleviate symptoms of certain mental disorders. I would currently most recommend the OmegaBrite brand, of which I take 2000 mg total a day,

half first thing then the rest before bed
4. Gingko Biloba: certain studies have claimed its usefulness in increasing concentration and memory; one minor side-effect is drowsiness
5. Exercise
6. Sleep (plan for rest when needed; if so, I take 0.75mg of Schiff Melatonin Plus before bed)
7. *Neuro Programmer 3* includes apparently intelligence raising sessions

WARNING! Please do not take my suggestions on food supplements for granted; if you are considering taking them, I would strongly advise consulting your doctor or other qualified professional first

SECONDARY BIBLIOGRAPHY (in roughly decreasing order of importance)

Gaston Bachelard	*The Poetics of Space* (Beacon Press, 1994)
Louis A. Bloomfield	*How Everything Works* (Wiley, 2007)
John Langone	*The New How Things Work* (National Geographic, 2004)
Marshall Brain	*How Stuff Works* (Chartwell Books, 2010) and *More How Stuff Works* (Wiley, 2002)

Chris Woodford, Ben Morgan, Clint Witchalls, Luke Collins and
Kevin Jones   *Cool Stuff And How It Works* (DK Children, 2009)

Mortimer Adler and Charles Lincoln Van Doren
    How To Read A Book (Touchstone, 1972)

Marc Auge and John Howe   *Non-Places* (Verso, 2009)

FORTHCOMING

(with Phil Chambers)   *A Guide To Memorising Mathematical and Scientific Formulae*

All text (completed Monday 19 December 2011) © James Timothy Smith